THE EMPOWERED MAMA

How to Reclaim Your Time and Yourself While Raising a Happy, Healthy Family

LISA DRUXMAN

Founder of FIT4MOM

FAIR WINDS

Inspiring | Educating | Creating | Entertaining

Brimming with creative inspiration, how-to projects, and useful information to enrich your everyday life, Quarto Knows is a favorite destination for those pursuing their interests and passions. Visit our site and dig deeper with our books into your area of interest: Quarto Creates, Quarto Cooks, Quarto Homes, Quarto Lives, Quarto Drives, Quarto Explores, Quarto Gifts, or Quarto Kids.

First Published in 2018 by Fair Winds Press, an imprint of The Quarto Group, 100 Cummings Center, Suite 265-D, Beverly, MA 01915, USA.
T (978) 282-9590 F (978) 283-2742 QuartoKnows.com

Fair Winds Press titles are also available at discount for retail, wholesale, promotional, and bulk purchase. For details, contact the Special Sales Manager by email at specialsales@quarto.com or by mail at The Quarto Group, Attn: Special Sales Manager, 401 Second Avenue North, Suite 310, Minneapolis, MN 55401, USA.

21 20 19 18 17   2 3 4 5

ISBN: 978-1-59233-770-5

Digital edition published in 2018
eISBN: 978-1-63159-445-8

Library of Congress Cataloging-in-Publication Data is available

Design: Allison Meierding
Illustration: Penelope Dullaghan

Printed in China

Contents

Foreword

I am honored and humbled that my wife Lisa asked me to write the foreword for her book. Well actually, she didn't ask me! She was looking at celebrities or experts and I jokingly offered to write it. To my surprise, she said yes! I'm guessing she did so because she wanted to convey our family values and introduce me as a first hand example to the benefits of this book.

Lisa and I have been married for over 20 years. She and I continue to grow together in our marriage based on many of the lessons she shares in this book. We have done these activities together and it's helped me as much as it's helped her. If you think your husband would never participate, you might be surprised. I am neither Mr. Communicator nor Mr. Sensitive, but this really does work and has been invaluable to our success.

Lisa has been and continues to be my inspiration to be a better person by keeping me true to my values and remaining focused on what's important in life.

When our son was born over 16 years ago, she went on a mission to create a career that allowed her to also be a mom. She continued that mission when she wanted to share that career with thousands of women across the country. But it was more than a job. Lisa found that moms were so busy taking care of everyone else that they forgot how to take care of themselves. Lisa adamantly believed that moms were the best model for a family's health—most moms just didn't know how to take care of everyone else and themselves. That's why she wrote this book.

I have been fortunate enough to be a part of this mission and witness many of the wonderful and amazing moms that Lisa has had the honor of working with, learning from and sharing in their success and sometimes grief. Lisa has never wavered in this mission and her passion continues to inspire moms. In this book, Lisa shares how she figured out how to take care of herself and how you can too. As a husband, I can tell you that we want you to be happy and healthy. I can vouch that Lisa is not perfect, but that she works hard every day to take care of herself and her family. And when she does, she sets out a ripple effect that impacts her family, her friends, and her community.

— Jason N. Druxman
Chief Founding Dad
Fit4Mom, LLC

Introduction

Do you want your children to take care of themselves the way you do?
Do you want them to eat like you do?
Do you want them to exercise like you do?
Do you want them to stress like you do?

I have asked thousands of moms these questions. And the answer is almost always NO. Moms want their kids to take better care of themselves, eat healthier, exercise more, and stress less.

Guess what? Teaching your kids how to do those things starts with you! You cannot wish it for them. You need to become their model mom, as in their role-model mom.

How about this question: *How are you?* Ask any mom and the answer goes something like this: "Crazy!" "Overwhelmed!" "So busy!"

In my book, "so busy" is not a badge of honor. If we want our kids to have great answers to questions about self-care and happiness, it is up to us as moms to set them up for success. Moms are catalysts for change. They are the model for the rest of the family. They are the foundation for healthy habits. The good news is that when mom takes care of herself, eats better, and exercises more—her family does, too. Not only that, a mom who takes good care of herself also answers that last question differently. She isn't overwhelmed. She is happy. She is healthy.

We have all heard the flight-safety guidance about putting on your own oxygen mask before your children's. We have all heard that we are supposed to follow that same philosophy as moms. I think that most moms believe this to be true—but NO ONE acts on it. I believe that's simply because most moms don't know how. Moms are so busy just surviving, and so overwhelmed with getting through the day-to-day, that they can't figure out how to take care of themselves.

That's what this book is about. It's about putting "me" before motherhood. It's not about being selfish, though. It's about the importance of giving the people in your family the best gift that they could ever have—happy, healthy, well-balanced lives. To do that, we have to live the way we want our children to live.

To laugh more, and to feel overwhelmed less.
To exercise more, and to run errands less.
To eat healthier, and to have fast food less.
To chill out more, and to stress less.

*Your children will follow your example,
not your advice.*

—AUTHOR UNKNOWN, BUT HE OR SHE IS DEFINITELY
A PARENT TO KNOW THIS TRUTH!

It seems to me that a happy life would be a pretty great legacy to leave your children. And I am going to walk you through exactly how to do it, step by step. Keep in mind that there is never a perfect balance, and I won't paint you pictures of perfect homes behind white picket fences. (Perhaps I should say I won't paint pictures of perfect homes from Pinterest.) Here, I will share a path that has worked for me, and it will work for you most of the time.

What qualifies me to give this kind of advice? To start, I am mom to Jacob and Rachel, and I am wife to Jason. At the time of writing this book, Jacob is fifteen, Rachel is twelve, and Jason and I are about to celebrate twenty years of marriage. I am also the founder of FIT4MOM, a company that has brought Fit4Baby, Stroller Strides, and Body Back fitness programs to a million moms across America.

Let's start with my business. FIT4MOM evolved from a major a-ha moment. I was on a walk with my son when he was just a wee baby. It was one of our best hours of the day. We both loved getting outside, and I loved getting some exercise. At the time, I had been a fitness professional for more than ten years, and I was thinking about how all moms want to get their bodies back after having a baby. In that moment, I realized that with my training I could help moms get their bodies back—using something that is already part of their lives *and* a great workout tool.

That's how I created the Stroller Strides workout. I started with a few moms in my neighborhood. At that point, I wasn't thinking about it as a business. I just needed support and community as a new mom. It was a big hit! Soon after that, my maternity leave was coming to an end, and I was devastated at the idea of going back to work and leaving my new beautiful baby. So, I decided to turn Stroller Strides into a business.

I wrote a budget to show my husband that if I offered a certain number of classes and got a certain number of members that we would be okay with that as my income. He was onboard, so I quit my job and started my life as an entrepreneur. I opened twelve locations in that first year and signed on 1,000 participants. I hired instructors, and I was teaching classes six days a week. There were so many women looking to get their bodies back and meet new moms. Word spread and the business took off—and this was before social media. I was getting emails from across the country from women who either wanted to start a class or join one.

Two years later we started testing the business model to see if it would be as successful in other cities and states. The model was a huge success in San Diego, but would the classes also work in other cities? We sold six "beta" licenses to see if the program had legs. We wanted to see if Stroller Strides worked in hot places, such as Arizona in the summer, and in cold places, such as New Jersey in the winter. And it did! We eventually franchised the business.

As my family grew up, so did the business. We added more programs, such as Fit4Baby and Body Back. And we aren't just classes. We are an incredible community of moms. We also have a blog, a podcast, retail goods, and more. We launched our own fitness stroller with BOB strollers. I wrote a book and created a DVD workout series called *Mama Wants Her Body Back*. We got a lot of great media exposure from the *Today Show*, *Good Morning America*, and more. We have been in virtually every fitness, business, and parenting magazine. And the best part is . . . I was a mom first and foremost the whole time.

We've had our share of hard times, but it's all been worth it. My proudest accomplishment has been creating hundreds of career opportunities that are supportive of motherhood.

Now let's talk about my personal life. I can honestly say that I think I am one of the happiest, healthiest moms I know. Whoa! That was scary to write. Worried about the haters, the judgers. But honestly, I think it's true. I have achieved all this, but I am not perfect. Far from it. I could write a whole chapter on my flaws. I just choose not to emphasize them because a negative focus doesn't serve any positive purpose. I have learned a lot about health, happiness, and motherhood during my own journey. I am walking my walk, and I am constantly striving to learn and grow as a person and a mom—and that's what I will share with you in this book.

I'm often asked how I came to have this lens on the world. Well first, I would like to give my parents a lot of credit. They have been an unconditional love in my life, and they have always had incredible belief in their daughters.

I can't be sure, but I think that my perspective may also have to do with a childhood incident that may have been a turning point in my life. When I was about thirteen years old, I got out of the car with my dad in a dark parking lot. A man came from the darkness, and I thought he was asking the time. He wasn't. I walked right into the barrel of his gun. He told us to get on the ground and hand over our belongings.

Most people say they see their life pass before them at moments like that. I didn't have much of a life at the time. I was only thirteen. So I saw the life I wasn't going to have. I wasn't going to get to go to college or get married or have kids. You see, it's times like that when you can quickly and clearly understand what's most important. At the end of your life, no matter when that comes, you won't be thinking about the errands you didn't run. You won't be thinking about Facebook or your inbox. You will be reflecting on the loves of your life.

At thirteen, I already had regrets. If that had been my last day, I would have left with a life of disappointments. Back then I was not at all the person I am today. I was living a life of can't. I did terribly in school. (I later found out that I had ADD, which explained a lot.) I was socially awkward and I had very few friends. I was terrible in sports. (Yep, I was that last person picked every time.) That was naturally who I was. But then I made it worse because I stopped trying. I didn't try in school or with friends or in sports because I believed I couldn't do it.

But after that incident in the parking lot, I slowly started to change my life of cant's. Maybe subconsciously I felt I was given a second chance. I started to try. I started making an effort in all areas of my life. If something was overwhelming, I would cut it down to bites I could swallow. When I was assigned a book to read in school, I took it a chapter at a time. It was still overwhelming. So I broke it into a paragraph at a time. Still overwhelming. So I broke it down to one sentence at a time.

And that's how I did it. I made small efforts that built up to a later success. And do you know what happened? I started to get better in all areas of my life. I started to build my confidence. I realized, why not me? Why shouldn't I be able to do it?

It does not matter if you are a natural at anything. If it means enough to you, you can learn and do almost anything. You just need to do it one baby step at a time. Think for a moment about a fitness or diet goal you have had in the past that you did not reach. Chances are that you did too much, too hard, too fast. Go slowly. Absorb some content and put it into action. Make it a habit. Make it part of your life. And then move to the next goal.

The balancing act of work and motherhood has been the hardest of my life. I have fallen off many times, and I want to share with you the lessons I learned so that you can learn from my path. My hope is to provide you with a toolbox that unlocks a life of happy and healthy motherhood.

I am writing this book with the hope of becoming a part of your life for the next year. Think of this as a journey we take together. As you read, break up the suggestions however you need to. When a plane takes off from one point and flies to another, it does not travel in a perfect line—it flies a little under, a little over, until it gets to the destination. I have been told that pilots are actually off track ninety percent of the time. Read this book as if I am taking you on a journey from an overwhelming life to a life with passion and purpose. From chaos to counterbalance. When you get off track, gently bring yourself back. It's part of the journey.

We are what we repeatedly do.
Excellence, then, is not an act, but a habit.

—WILL DURANT

Secrets of Success

My girlfriends tease me because I'm always asking them what their secrets are. *What's your secret to a happy marriage? What's your secret to being healthy? What's your secret to staying so organized?* I believe that success leaves clues, and people who are successful have a secret that must be shared...I guess I'm a success-clue hunter!

Have you heard the theory that you are the average of the five people you surround yourself with? Well, I try to surround myself with successful people so that I can learn from them. I'm not just talking about the people who are in my life. I'm talking about what I read and who I listen to every single day. I have learned from great leaders, such as Elizabeth Gilbert, John Maxwell, Michael Hyatt, Zig Ziglar, Anthony Robbins, Brené Brown, and others. I am bringing to you the tools and techniques that I have curated from them and use in my daily life.

And I do not *ever* stop learning. Every single day, I learn something new. I am a work in progress. We all are. And I have learned a lot of tips and tricks for being happy, healthy, and successful—that's what I want to share with you in this book. I bet if I sat down with you, you could teach me a thing or two. So I thank you for joining me on this journey, and I hope that some of my secrets to success (and the secrets I've learned from others) work for you!

Become a Life Master

We learn so much every single day. We process so much information, something to the tune of 174 newspapers a day in content. But processing information is not the same as mastering it. If I mastered all of the content I have processed from books and podcasts, I would be one of the great leaders of the world. Most information just goes in and out, and some of it gets stored as trivia or future quotations (if it's retained at all).

When it comes to the information in this book, I want you to master it. I want you to select what means the most to you and make it a part of your life. This takes intention and a plan *and* follow through. This book has been written in bite-size pieces: Take it in. Absorb what I've said. Then figure out how it may work in your life.

The book is written in a workbook style. If you want it to work, do the work! Carve out a little bit of time and actually write down the answers. If you only listen, you will only get surface results. There are lots of bullet points. Somehow, that's the easiest way for me to learn. I hope it works for you too! If you master what I share with you, you will be living intentionally every day.

Chapter 1

Focus on Yourself

We can only be a mother in relation to someone else. Did you notice that five-sixths of the word "mother" is "other"? So it's no wonder we moms often focus on everyone else before ourselves. In this chapter, I challenge you to be SELF-ish. By being self-ish, you'll be able to see how you want to live and you'll identify your values as the guiding principles in life—and for the life you'll design through this book.

Cultivate Your Self-ish Spirit

When did motherhood start meaning that you had to give up "me"? Most moms are so busy taking care of everyone else that they don't take care of themselves. Whether they simply forget or, like martyrs, refuse to make themselves a priority, the result is the same: drained, harried, stressed, way-too-busy, overtired moms. Is that really helping *any*one?

If you were a cell phone, how charged would your screen say your battery is? Would it be flashing red, telling you that you need to plug in? I imagine a world where moms have indicator lights on their foreheads and we are all blinking low battery.

There is no rule that says you have to give up your sense of yourself in order to be a mom. Quite the contrary, actually. If you can find, protect, and nourish the "me" in mommy, you become a better mom. I know what you're thinking, but no, this is not about being extremely selfish, claiming *all* the time and attention for yourself. This is about claiming *some* time and attention for yourself. It is about being self-*ish*: taking enough time for yourself to keep you going and to give you more strength for mother-hood . . . and beyond.

In my job, moms most often want help with their fitness, food, time management, and work. But if I could help moms with only one thing, it would be this: getting each mom to take care of her own spirit. I am so saddened by seeing moms in a constant state of feeling overwhelmed. I am beyond frustrated with seeing moms spread thin and exhausted, using food or alcohol to fill a void. This is not a martyr's badge of honor, moms. This is a problem. Your family needs you to show up as your best self.

The good news is that the problem can be fixed. Quite easily, actually. All you need to do is to take a little purposeful time to feel good throughout your day. Here are a few activities to get you started.

WAYS TO TAKE A ME BREAK

- Walk
- Meditate
- Journal
- Pray
- Exercise
- Stretch
- Breathe
- Doodle
- Read
- Take a bath
- Aromatherapy
- Light a candle
- Get in nature
- Unplug from your electronic devices
- Play relaxing music
- Learn
- Take a nap

How can you possibly fit even one self-care activity into each day? Just do it. Make the time. Make it a priority the way you do with all the activities you do every day for your family.

A break doesn't require much. Stop to tune in to your inner thoughts. Focus on your breath. Daydream for a moment. Set the timer on your phone and do something to recharge—even if it's only for a few minutes a few times a day. Even if you only start with once a day.

If you do this, something magical will happen. The more you slow down, the more time you will have. You will find that you aren't turning toward food or some bad habit as a quick fix. You will find that you react to the next tantrum with compassion instead of a cringe. You will start to create an energy around you that brings peace and happiness, even in the busiest of days.

Self-ish exercise

When was the last time you did something for yourself?

_____

_____

_____

_____

_____

_____

What did you do?

_____

_____

_____

_____

_____

How did it affect your day?

_____

_____

_____

_____

_____

_____

_____

If you make sure that your spiritual battery is charged, you will be ready for the chaos of the day. Yes, it will take some practice to get used to regularly charging your own battery. So stick with me in this book, and I will give you plenty of tips and tools to help!

COMMIT TO YOURSELF

If I asked you to do something today to give yourself a recharge break, would you be all in, diving in with both feet to make it happen? Or would you hesitate, thinking things like "maybe" or "if there's time"? Well, we both know that *maybe* usually means *no* and there won't be enough time, so you need a different tactic.

It's time to **commit to yourself** and use that solid mom backbone and determination. Insist on giving yourself time to be self-ish every single day. Commit to your health, physically and spiritually. For your family and for yourself.

One of the strongest ways to show a commitment is to sign a pledge. Are you ready? It's okay if you're not sure. I wrote this book to help you make and keep your commitment, so you are not alone. You've got this!

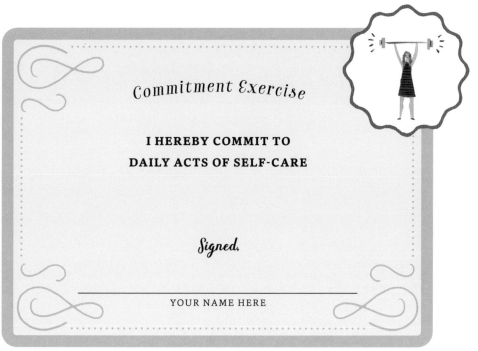

Commitment Exercise

**I HEREBY COMMIT TO
DAILY ACTS OF SELF-CARE**

Signed,

_____

YOUR NAME HERE

GIVE YOURSELF PERMISSION

You've made this commitment to yourself and that's fantastic! Now, there's one more thing you might need to give yourself: *permission*. Permission to give your own needs a vote in each day. Permission to take time for you (and only you). In other words, give yourself permission to put the "me" back in mommy.

Most of us can see the value in caring for our spirits and our bodies, but we don't follow through because we don't give ourselves permission to be self-ish. Let's get that out of your way right now. And, if you're having a hard time with the idea, remember this is actually a gift you are giving to your family!

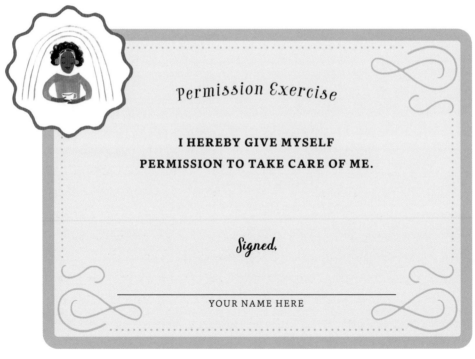

Permission Exercise

**I HEREBY GIVE MYSELF
PERMISSION TO TAKE CARE OF ME.**

Signed,

_____
YOUR NAME HERE

Congratulations! You've already taken two big steps towards a more fully healthy life for yourself *and* your family.

Legacy, Part 1

At the end of your life, how do you want to be remembered? How do you want to be remembered as a mom? What do you want your kids to say about you? Feel about you? Do you think you are on track for that kind of eulogy?

Bummer of a topic to start a book with, isn't it? I know it isn't the most uplifting topic, but this is one of the most powerful, no-nonsense ways to look at your life. I use it daily.

At the end of your life, you will ask yourself if you are proud of how you lived. You will look back at how you played the cards that you were dealt. You will reminisce on the places you went and the relationships you built. You will remember the obstacles you conquered and the struggles you overcame. And you may also wonder what kind of legacy you are leaving behind.

What I am calling your attention to here is actually not about your death. It's about your *life* and how you will use it from this moment forward. Our time here is finite, so let's look that fact square in the face and decide to live with intention every day. I regularly use this perspective myself, asking those tough life-and-death questions to help stay clear on my priorities.

We must be careful because so much of daily life has nothing to do with those times you'll look back on at the end. You won't remember how many emails you sorted through or how many Facebook friends you had. You won't be proud of that laundry mess you vanquished instead of playing jacks on the floor with your kids. You won't look back fondly on the times that you blamed or complained. In fact, you might look back to realize that the legacy you created is not the one you hoped for.

Life is very uncertain. I know we don't like to think about it, but tomorrow—or even today—could be our last day. From this perspective, life is no longer about being perfect. It's about handling your challenges with some semblance of grace. It's about living on purpose. It's about getting back up when you fall down. It's about hugging deeply and loving purely. It's about family, friends, forgiveness, taking chances, and paying it forward. And it's about taking care of yourself. These are all things you can do right here and now to create a life without regrets.

No Regrets Exercise

At the end of your life, what might you regret not having done?

_____

_____

_____

_____

_____

_____

_____

_____

Keep this in mind as you go through the life-planning exercises in this book. No regrets.

VALUES

Our time with our children is so incredibly short and our chance to influence their lives is fleeting, even if we all live long, healthy lives. Our legacy is the thing that can keep affecting our children (and their children, too) long after our physical presence is gone. So let's be intentional about it.

To set your desired legacy in motion, you need to know who you are. You may think you already know that, using labels like *mother* or *wife* or *sister* or *employee*. But who are you underneath those labels? Who are you at your core? What matters the most to you and gives you the most joy? What provides you with the reasons for doing what you do and being who you are? In other words, what are your values?

> *It's not hard to make decisions once you know what your values are.*
>
> **—ROY DISNEY**

Your values represent your guiding principles. When you are in tune with what is most important to you, the path of your life becomes clearer and it is easier to set priorities. Deep down, your values will tell you if you are on track.

From my own page . . . I've read lots of books that have asked me to fill stuff out. I rarely do it. I'm too busy. I always think I've got the concept and that I don't need to take the time. I was wrong. When you take the time to write it down, it creates a connection to your brain that will help solidify the concept. If you are ready to get out of being overwhelmed, do the work! Trust me!

Values Exercise, Part 1

Below is a list of value words. This is not even close to a full list. That could fill a book! Read through the list, and then answer the following questions.

Acceptance	Courage	Faithful
Accomplishment	Curiosity	Family
Achievement	Daring	Fearless
Adventure	Dedication	Fierce
Affection	Determined	Flexible
Altruism	Devotion	Focused
Appreciation	Different	Freedom
Balance	Diversity	Friendly
Beauty	Down-to-earth	Fun
Boldness	Dreamer	Generous
Brilliance	Encouragement	Giving
Calmness	Effective	Good
Caring	Elegant	Gratitude
Confident	Enthusiastic	Happiness

Harmony	Maturity	Serenity
Health	Mindful	Spiritual
Hopeful	Motivation	Silliness
Humble	Optimism	Stillness
Humor	Passion	Strength
Innovative	Patient	Talent
Insightful	Persistent	Teamwork
Joyful	Positive	Tolerance
Kindness	Productive	Understanding
Knowledge	Purpose	Virtue
Learning	Relaxation	Vision
Leadership	Resilience	Vitality
Love	Respect	Winning
Loyalty	Risk	Wonder
Mastery	Security	

Pick the top ten values that match the core of your being. If you didn't see your value word, feel free to add it below.

1. _____
2. _____
3. _____
4. _____
5. _____
6. _____
7. _____
8. _____
9. _____
10. _____

Now it gets a little more difficult. From the list of ten, pick your top three core values.

1. _____

2. _____

3. _____

Now we get really tough. Imagine you were getting a tattoo to represent your number one core value. What would the tattoo be?

_____

_____

_____

_____

What Is Your #1 Core Value?

_____

_____

Remember that word. Write it down, and keep it in front of you (tattoo optional). Why? Your core values can help you in all decisions, from work to family. They should match your heart and your behaviors. For example, if family is in your top three, but you work seventy hours a week, there is a contradiction in how you are living. You will feel stress and conflict as a result of that mismatch.

Look again at your top three core values. Do they make you feel good? Do they represent who you want to be? You should be proud of your values. If your list doesn't energize you, replace the duds with values that truly speak to you.

This is the time—right here and now—to live by design, not by default. This is the time to be the real you. This is the time to build your legacy!

Values Exercise, Part 2

Re-create your list of ten value words in a form that you can keep near you throughout each day. Make sure to differentiate the importance of the values, so you can see the top three and the number one most important value at a glance.

Do this in whatever way works best for you. For instance, create your values list on the computer and save it as an image for your phone's background. Print it and put it next to your computer, on the back of your medicine cabinet, and on the refrigerator. You want to tap into your values every single day. They are the design for your life.

SECURE YOUR SUPPORT

Becoming a mom can be a very lonely experience. You expect it to be joyous and chock full of happiness but it can actually be very isolating. You're exhausted. You don't know how to care for this little bundle. And you are alone.

But really, you have just joined the most ancient of communities . . . motherhood. All moms are connected. All moms want to support one another. Find your village. I started Stroller Strides so I could have my own village. Find a meet-up or a group near you. You are not alone. And there are other moms who want to be there for you.

From my own page . . . I didn't want to share my values with you until you had a chance to do your own work. I hope you didn't skip ahead. There is so much pressure to feel like we should be like others. Honor the values you chose. They may change at different times of your life. My top three right now are: love, health, and time. Seems to me that when I live from love, all is good! Health is a foundation of my life. And time is a consistently high value for me. I value time and realize how precious it is!

Monthly Challenge

January:
Commit to nourishing the ME in mommy.
Take ten minutes each day to recharge.

Stop striving for perfection. Strive to be better than you were yesterday.
Don't just go through this year. Grow through it!

Chapter 2

Find Your Purpose

Now that you are charged up and ready to create positive changes in your life, it's time to get clear about what you want that life to look like. In this chapter, I will help you get started on designing your life—after we get serious about your dreams.

Dreams / Vision

When you were a kid, you probably painted pictures in your head of what you wanted your life to look like. I thought I would be an artist or maybe that lady that twirled from ropes in the circus. Never did my parents tell me that my dreams would not happen. My daughter, Rachel, is imagining that she will be a veterinarian and a teacher. My son Jacob is imagining having an indoor basketball court and bowling alley in his house. I'm not one to squash any dreams, so we support those ideas with plans. I will help you do the same.

First, you need know what your dreams are. You can't build a solid plan on a vague idea! We often talk about being clear on goals for things such as losing weight or accomplishing something at work. But what about what you want your life to look like, feel like? What do you dream of doing? Do you have a clear vision of that? And when do you want it to happen? (As my friend Annie Fonte says, "Someday is not on any calendar.")

I find it interesting that the moms I talk with most often want more time to exercise, more time for self, and more time in nature—not things that cost money, such as fancy houses or cars. So if you're using money as an excuse for not getting clear about your dreams, you'll need to find a different reason . . . or maybe just do the following exercise.

Dreams Exercise

Take a few minutes to write down your dreams, whether you think they are realistic or not. Create a vivid picture of what a successful, happy life would look like for you. In your dream life, where are you living? Who is around you? What are you doing? What is a perfect day like? And how does it all feel? Write down as much detail as you can. Remember, there are no obstacles in this dream.

Wheel of Life

Dreams are all well and good, but how can we turn them into something real? Zig Ziglar, author and motivational speaker, said: "If you can dream it, you can achieve it." I absolutely believe that, and I will show you how you can make that true for you.

One of my favorite tools is the Wheel of Life. It looks at different areas of your life as one whole picture with the following sections:

- Career
- Social
- Financial
- Family
- Physical
- Mental
- Spiritual

You assess each area of your life as it is right now, and you chart your rating on a "wheel" (see opposite) to get a quick snapshot of how balanced your life is. A wheel should be round, but when you fill out this assessment you will probably realize that your wheel is a little (or a lot!) off-kilter. We all tend to focus more heavily on certain areas of our life, perhaps completely neglecting other important ones. The first step to bringing those areas of your life closer to a balance is to take an honest look at where you put most of your time and attention.

Wheel of Life Exercise, part 1

Take a look at the different areas of your life from finance to romance. Rate them from 1 to 10 (10 being highest satisfaction) by putting a big dot on the line beside that number. After you've rated all the areas, draw a line from one dot to the next, the whole way around the wheel. What is the shape you end up with after you connect those dots? The ideal balance forms a large circle, but chances are that your life looks like a more jagged shape that probably wouldn't roll very well. That's how it feels when some areas of your life are out of balance, doesn't it?

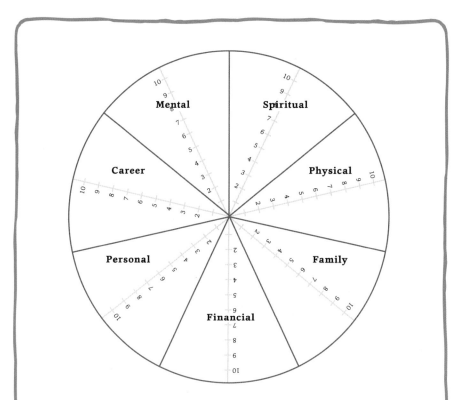

Let's take a closer look at your wheel.

What low-scoring area causes the most angst in your gut? That's the area to focus on with a plan to raise its score. Don't worry, I'll walk you through that process later in this chapter, but you can start right away by carving out a bit of time to learn, plan, or play with a focus on that area.

What high-scoring area gives you the most joy? Pat yourself on the back for creating satisfaction in that area!

The Wheel of Life is a tool to help you live on purpose. An ideal life might be a smooth, round wheel, but it's quite possible that your ideal life looks nothing like that. Maybe you are okay with a little less fun and a little more financial stability. Maybe you are fine with less career satisfaction if that means you have more time and energy for the other areas of your life. There is no right or wrong answer, just make it an intentional choice. It's your life!

(continued on next page)

My friendship score has been low for a while, and I'm at peace with it. This stage of my life is more focused on my family and my business. I had a low score in the financial area. That was not okay with me. I'm not just talking about wanting more money. I felt that I needed to have more knowledge about retirement and college savings. So, I started learning and committed to reading three books last year on financial freedom.

Keep in mind that our lives change through the years. I recommend doing this Wheel of Life exercise at least once a year.

Now that you have an overall picture of your life satisfaction, let's dig into a mom's favorite topic: TIME.

Time Inventory Exercise (Wheel of Life, part 2)

Fill in the form below with the average number of hours you spend in each area each day. How much time are you currently spending in these areas? How much time do you want to spend?

TIME SPENT

	Now	Desire
Work		
Marriage/Love		
Sleeping		
Fun		
Household		
Children		
Religion		
Phone/Email		
Exercise		

Many of my clients say that their Now score adds up to more than twenty-four hours in a day! Sure feels like that doesn't it?

Compare the amount of time spent on each area with the level of satisfaction you rated on your Wheel of Life. Is there a correlation? This is a bit of a chicken-and-egg situation: Sometimes we spend time on something because we are happy with how it's going. Sometimes we are happy with how something is going, so we spend more time on it. Either way, you can get a good idea here of where you might want to put more of your time and attention.

For starters, pick three areas from your Wheel of Life that don't have the score you want. What is one thing you can do, starting today, to shift the balance a little toward what you desire in those areas?

Write down those three changes and put them where you will see them each day so you don't forget your commitment! You can use this as a template.

1. *Area:* _____

_____

Change I'll make: _____

_____

_____

_____

2. *Area:* _____

_____

Change I'll make: _____

_____

_____

_____

3. *Area:* _____

_____

Change I'll make: _____

_____

_____

_____

Personal Action Plan

Now that you have a clearer picture of the life you want, and where some areas might be out of balance, you need a plan to bring it all together. Let's design that life and make a plan!

Well it's not a daydream
if you decide to make it your life

—"SHE'S ON FIRE" BY TRAIN

Take a few minutes to reread your description of your dream life, then review your Wheel of Life and your Time Inventory. From that picture you painted for yourself, let's start to break it down into levels. (Remember the baby steps?)

Level 1: The ultimate dream, whether you think it's possible or not. (Example: owning a ranch with horses)
Level 2: A reach, but possible with a plan. (Example: renting a house in Italy for a week)
Level 3: A nonnegotiable must-have for your life. (Example: being able to send my kids to college)

Using these levels, decide which parts of your dreams fit in each level and write them below. By the way, those three examples are my own personal ones!

Level 1: _____

_____

Level 2: _____

_____

Level 3: _____

_____

Your Personal Action Plan

A dream written down with a date becomes a goal.
A goal broken down into steps becomes a plan.
A plan backed by action makes your
dreams come true.

—GREG S. REID

Starting with the smallest chunk (Level 3), write down a goal for each level, filling in the details below. For example, if sending your kids to college is your goal, then maybe the first step is to figure out how much money you will need. The second step might be to figure out how much you would need to put away each month. The third step may be to look at your finances and figure out where you can make adjustments. Don't worry about how you will have the time or energy to do these things. I'll help you with that in the rest of this book!

Goal Level 3

Make It SMART (Specific, Measurable, Achievable, Realistic, Timely)

SMART goal:

_____

_____

By when?

_____

_____

Why do I want to accomplish this goal?

_____

_____

_____

_____

How will I feel if I don't accomplish this goal?

_____

_____

_____

_____

Break it down. What will you need to do to accomplish this goal?
(Feel free to add more steps, if necessary.)

1. _____

2. _____

3. _____

4. _____

5. _____

_____

_____

_____

Goal Level 2

Make It SMART (Specific, Measurable, Achievable, Realistic, Timely)

SMART goal:

_____

_____

By when?

_____

_____

Why do I want to accomplish this goal?

_____

_____

_____

_____

How will I feel if I don't accomplish this goal?

_____

_____

_____

_____

Break it down. What will you need to do to accomplish this goal?
(Feel free to add more steps, if necessary.)

1. _____

2. _____

3. _____

4. _____

5. _____

_____

_____

_____

Goal Level 1

Make It SMART (Specific, Measurable, Achievable, Realistic, Timely)

SMART goal:

_____

_____

By when?

_____

_____

Why do I want to accomplish this goal?

_____

_____

_____

How will I feel if I don't accomplish this goal?

_____

_____

_____

Break it down. What will you need to do to accomplish this goal?

(Feel free to add more steps, if necessary.)

1. _____
2. _____
3. _____
4. _____
5. _____

_____

_____

Monthly Challenge

february:

Choose one section of your Wheel of Life that scored lower than you'd like. Give it ten more minutes of time each day.

Stop striving for perfection. Strive to be better than you were yesterday.
Don't just go through this year. Grow through it!

Chapter 3
Make More Time

Are you over scheduled? Squeezing activities into every single moment? Every mom hopes for more hours in the day, but I doubt much would change if that twenty-fifth hour was added. What we need instead is an awareness of how we use our time, and ways to simplify what we do with the time we have. This chapter will help you evaluate what you want to commit to most, so you accomplish what matters most, first. It will also teach you how to delegate certain projects and how to create a village of moms where you all help each other!

Prioritize

*Time is a created thing. To say "I don't have time"
is like saying "I don't want to."*

—LAO TZU

Almost every mom I meet seems frantic and overwhelmed, wearing *busy* like it's a Girl Scout badge. Take a breath. No, really, stop take a deep breath right now. Slow down. It's not that easy, you say? I know. Believe me, I know! I, too, was that person running so fast, all the time. Truth be told, I still am. But I have put myself through rigorous training to get out of being overwhelmed and into a slower, more peaceful life. I'll help you do the same.

How many times have you wished for more hours in the day? *Poof!* I've just given you three more hours. How would you use them? Would you exercise more? Meditate? Play? I doubt it. I suspect your mind went right to your to do list, getting more chores and day-to-day tasks done. And anyway, having more time is just a fantasy, right?

Wrong. The truth is that we have all been given more time. Think about how much time technology has given us through efficiencies. We don't have to get up to turn the channel on the television. (Yes, I am that old.) We can order things online and barely ever go to the store. We have fast food. Fast phones. Fast cars. Fast lives. So yes, we have been given more time, but the problem is that we fill those hours with the same old stuff. Stuff that does not feed our souls.

Most of us get through our day by reacting. We wake up, we make meals, do laundry, drive kids places, go to work. We live off a never-ending to do list, getting done what seemingly has to get done. That's right, I said *seemingly*. Some of what you do might not actually need to get done. Or at least it might not have to get done by you. Something to think about. (I'll talk more about delegating later in this chapter.)

Time is free, but it's priceless.
You can't own it, but you can use it.
You can't keep it, but you can spend it.
Once you've lost it you can never get it back.

—HARVEY MACKAY

MITs

We all have the same 24 hours in a day and 168 hours in a week. They will go by no matter how you plan to use them, so we need to choose how we use those hours. I learned that the hard way.

A few years into my business, I was the one running around frantically with my head cut off. Until my sister confronted me about it. She said that I always seemed stressed, and I didn't have time for family or friends. Ironically, I didn't have time to enjoy my kids—and that was the reason I started my business in the first place! Slap. Ouch. Honesty like only a sister can share. But she was so right about all of it.

I knew things had to change. So, I sat down at my desk and looked over my to do list, which at that time was still on paper. It was pages long and most of it had nothing to do with what was important to me. Instead, it was a list of work and errands, more work and more errands. I stopped right then and figured out the three most important areas of my life. At that time, they were family, business, and friends. I realized that I needed to alter that because the energy I was putting into family was just my kids; my marriage needed more attention, too.

So, I changed my list. I started making my list based on what was important to me. I called them my **M**ost **I**mportant **T**hings (MITs). That activity was transformational for me, and I want to share it with you.

MITs Exercise

Take another long, deep breath. Close your eyes and clear your head. What are the three most important areas of your life? I know there are many important areas, but what are the three most *important?*

1. _____

2. _____

3. _____

Now take a look at your current to do list. How much of it ties in with your three most important areas?

Re-write your to do list, including only tasks that tie into your MITs. Did you find yourself saying, "No, wait, I can't take THAT off my list!"? My challenge to you is to go ahead and remove those things from your list.

Next, put your MITs (Most Important Things) in the three large circles to the left (one per circle).

Now, fill in that middle with ME!

You cannot take care of those other areas of your life if you aren't taking care of you.

Remember the commitment you made to yourself in chapter 1? It's time to put that into practice.

TAKE CARE OF ME

What can you do every single day to take care of you, whether you think you have time or not? Here's a list to get your thoughts flowing.

1. *Take a walk*
2. *Meditate*
3. *Get in nature*
4. *Write in your journal*
5. *Eat your veggies*
6. *Drink your water*
7. *Take your vitamins*
8. *Take a yoga class*
9. *Go for a run (or jog or crawl)*
10. *Take a fitness class*
11. *Read an inspiring (or just interesting!) book*
12. _____
13. _____
14. _____
15. _____

I have come up with a little "me" checklist that keeps me feeling charged. Every day I need to check off these items.

- ☐ **Move.** Every day I need to move. Ideally, this means some form of exercise, but walking the dog counts, too!
- ☐ **Fuel.** Every day I want to fuel myself with good whole foods.
- ☐ **Reflect.** Every day I want to take a bit of time to reflect on my goals, how I'm feeling, and what I'm grateful for.
- ☐ **Be.** Every day I want to take ten minutes to just be. This may consist of meditation, journaling, or just resting.
- ☐ **Learn.** Every day I want to learn. This is usually in the form of audiobooks and podcasts.

Who has time for this? You do!

If you were to write down your own "me" checklist, what would be on it?

1. _____

2. _____

3. _____

4. _____

5. _____

There are different seasons of your life, and your MITs will change depending on your season. Keep your list fresh!

Put a "Take Care of ME" list like this one somewhere that you will see it every day! When you start your day, choose what you will do for each of your MITs each day, including you!

For instance, if my MITs are my kids, my marriage, and my business (with me in the middle), then my MITs for the day might look like:

Play a board game with my kids (without looking at my phone while we play).

Send my husband a randy text to let him know I'm thinking of him.

I do more than one MIT a day for my business! Who are we kidding?

However, I can still pick the most important task of the day.

Take ten minutes for myself to meditate and take care of ME.

I find that there is always too much to do. If I pull back and focus on what the most important things are, then I am always on track.

You can use your MITs to figure out the three most important areas of your life. AND, it's also helpful to focus on three MITs each day. That is your to do list—to always get done what's most important! This is a key to avoid being overwhelmed and, at the same time, remain focused in your life of purpose.

Simplify and Prune

Fact: We are too busy. Our time and our brains are on overload. Doing a few breathing exercises, important as they are, is not going to magically free up our jam-packed lives. We need to cut back and strip down. We need to simplify. Do you have to be the team mom, room parent, *and* cookie bake sale chef extraordinaire? No. Does your child need to be in three sports and an afterschool tutoring program? No.

Think about your closet. When you buy a new shirt or a new pair of shoes, you put them in your closet. Do you then remove an old pair of shoes and shirt? Probably not. I'm guessing you keep adding things. But what if you never take anything out? Your closet will end up bursting at the seams. In that overloaded mess, you can't even see what you have.

Let's look at another example. You probably know that the most beautiful rose bushes are the ones that are carefully pruned. A rosebush creates more flowers than it can sustain, so the gardener needs to prune back the good blooms to make more room for the best blooms.

Sometimes our lives need pruning, too. Where in your life do you have too much going on? Where is your life so packed full that you can't see or pay much attention to what's in there? It's time to prune some activities. It may be painful to cut back, but it is the only way to make room for what is most important to you. It's no longer okay to try to do everything yourself. It's time to be wisely selective.

Sometimes gardeners prune a plant to remove unhealthy parts, such as a dead branch or diseased leaves, because they can spread to make the whole plant sick. Where might there be some habits or activities that are weighing you down, threatening your health? Putting more energy into these situations isn't the answer. Maybe they served you in the past, but that season is over. The things that aren't working for you need to be cut away to make room for your happier, healthier life.

> *When we become skilled at selectively knowing what to prune out of our lives, what remains becomes stronger, brighter, clearer.*
>
> **—LISA BYRNE**

Sometimes it's people that we need to prune out of our lives. Like the great blooms of the rosebush, some people in your life energize and inspire you, making your world seem more manageable and enjoyable. Seek those people out and invite them into your days! Other people consistently drain you and sap your energy with their negativity and complaining. This might sound harsh, but you might need to prune those people from your life. You have no obligation to carry the weight of someone else's negativity, especially when you start feeling your own light dimming from the effort.

I try to surround myself with optimists.
I don't care how smart and clever people may be;
if they are addicted to a dark view of the world,
I don't want them in my house or anywhere near my
life. It's too heavy. For me, the most inspirational
people are the ones who put the shoulders up
against the wheel of despair and PUSH back really
hard—not just once, not just a few times in their
lives, but every single day.

—ELIZABETH GILBERT,
EXCERPT FROM AN INTERVIEW ON GOODREADS.COM

We all need to make exceptions for what I call the "necessary entry" people: those you have to spend time with because of their relationship to your work or your family. For example, I'm talking about your boss or your mother-in-law (not mine, of course). You can't just prune them out of your life, so you need to at least put an emotional barrier between yourself and those people. It is up to you to keep them from toxifying your time and energy.

Yes and No

Life is precious and finite, just like any season. You can't have everything and you can't do everything. To truly thrive, you need to be deliberate about what you nurture and what you cut back.

To prune with a purpose, you need to learn how to use two words more intentionally: yes and no. They are two words that you say all day every day, but do you realize how important they are to your life balance?

If you are anything like me, you say yes too often. Maybe it's because we don't want to miss out or maybe it's because we don't want to disappoint, but we just don't say no enough. We wind up overcommitted and stretched too thin. Do more. Do more. Do more. Until we are in a total state of madness.

Every time you say yes to one thing, you are saying no to something else. The fact is that your day is already full from the time you get up until the time you go to sleep. And I doubt it's filled with watching TV and eating bonbons all day. So before you say yes to something, ask yourself what you are willing *not* to do?

When I began my Motivating Mom podcast, I knew I needed to stop doing some other projects because my schedule was already full. I needed to figure out a way to delegate some tasks or to drop them altogether. I don't always want to say no, but I often know that I need to. I get emails almost every day from aspiring entrepreneurs who want to take me to coffee or lunch to pick my brain. I wish I could help every one of them. My heart wants to, but my time won't allow it. If I said yes to them, I would not have time for my most important things.

You don't have to be a working mom for this to apply to you. If your life feels full, you may need to say no to being the room mom or baking cookies for the bake sale. We tend to think of no as a negative word, but I think we moms should use it more often—for ourselves. A "no" will keep things off your plate, allowing you to simplify and prune your life. You must learn to say no because saying no can bring you freedom. I said no to doing the dishes by myself and to making my kids lunches. Guess what? It created room in my life.

Saying no doesn't have to only be reactive: saying no when someone else asks you to do something. Maybe you need to say no to what you don't want in your life. If your life feels too full or you don't have time to do what's important to you, what can you choose to say no to? Maybe you say no to cleaning the house and hire a housekeeper. Maybe you say no to having debt and stop buying daily lattes. Say no to having someone in your life who saps your energy. Say no to what you don't want. No to added stress, toxic people, and toxic food. My point is that no is a very powerful word. Don't confuse it with negativity. It can work for you or against you.

But what about the things you really do want to do? Isn't it okay to say yes to things, too? Yes! As long as you do it intentionally. You can create magic with yes, but it's a tricky word. If you use it too much, you get overwhelmed. If you don't use it enough, you lose your positive spark. What's tricky is that sometimes you need to say yes, even when you don't want to.

I remember many years ago I was invited to be a guest at the spa at Rancho La Puerta. When my friend invited me, my original inclination was to say no. I had just started dating my future husband, Jason, and I kind of wanted to hang at home with him. It would have been easier. But I am so glad that I didn't go for easy. That trip was amazing! It was a huge opportunity for me. Not only did I get to experience the spa, they started to invite me back as a guest instructor.

Saying yes when I want to say no comes up regularly for me. Truth be told, I'm probably an introvert. I have my best energy alone or in small groups. When I am invited to large networking meetings, it sounds pretty awful to me. But I say yes, because it brings me closer to what I want to achieve.

Say yes when a fear of failure is what's making you want to say no—taking that chance can give you opportunities like you've never known. Take advantage of opportunities when they come, even if timing isn't perfect or you don't feel ready. I have interviewed hundreds of entrepreneurs about their businesses and every single one said that they didn't feel ready when they started. Yes can lead you to new places, introduce you to new people, and help you abandon your fears.

Remember though, it's a balance. Really. There have been numerous times in the course of my career when I have been totally overwhelmed. I asked Jason for his patience because I had so much going on, but I was I was sure it would soon pass. He once said, "No it won't. Because you put yourself in this position. You keep saying yes to everything." And, as much as I hate to admit it, he was right. Just because something sounds like a good opportunity doesn't mean you have to say yes. Just because you can, doesn't mean you should. Ask yourself, will saying yes bring me happiness? Will saying yes bring me closer to achieving my MITs?

So how do you know when you should say yes and when you should say no? Before you agree to yet another commitment, stop and consider how the cost of the opportunity compares with its potential benefits? We make trade-offs in life. I have traded time with friends for time with family and business. I carve out some time for my girlfriends, but I say no to them far more than I say yes. I feel bad to let them down, but I know that overcommitting does me no good. I realize the commitment has to be to my kids and my business at this stage of my life. That trade-off might not be right for you. I just want you to realize that a little no in your life may bring you a lot of peace.

Being alive requires that we sometimes kill off things in which we were once invested, uproot what we previously nurtured, and tear down what we built for an earlier time.

—HENRY CLOUD

Yes and No Exercise

In his book Essentialism: The Disciplined Pursuit of Less, *Greg McKeown shares a mind-set of focusing on what is truly essential in your life. It's about getting the right things done and only doing what truly matters. It's about doing less, but better, in our lives. I think it's about time that you start saying YES to what's essential and saying NO to the noise.*

Let's get real here and put this idea into practice.

What MITs am I committed to doing?

_____

_____

> **What am I doing that I shouldn't?**
>
> _____
>
> _____
>
> **Who am I spending time with that I shouldn't?**
>
> _____
>
> _____
>
> *Now use your answers to guide your time management. Prioritize your MITs and prune out the parts of your life that keep you from them.*

*Remember that if you don't prioritize
your life, someone else will.*

—GREG MCKEOWN

Yes and no might be the two most powerful words in your vocabulary. They can create new realities. My hope is that you use them wisely. Say no to keep out what you don't want—and to keep focused on what you do want. Say yes to living your life on purpose!

Moms Need to Delegate!

Most moms are simply doing too much. Our days are not nine-to-five. Our days are from the minute we open our eyes until the minute we close them at night. And those days... well, we pack those days, don't we? Play dates and errands, laundry and cooking, cleaning and driving (Oh, the driving!). Maybe you work, too. Well it's no wonder we are overwhelmed.

The average stay-at-home mom works 96.5 hours per week. Don't believe me? Go to salary.com and check. There is even a calculator so you can see what your salary would be if you did that work for a company. Once you calculate your salary, it might make sense for you to be the Chief Executive Officer of your family—instead of the Chief Everything Officer.

What's the difference? A Chief Executive Officer delegates. A Chief Everything Officer does everything herself. To move toward a little more margin in our value as CMEO (Chief Mom Executive Officer), we must delegate.

What do you think of when you hear that word delegate? That you don't have anyone to delegate to? Or you don't have time to teach someone to do what you need? Or you can't afford to delegate? Or (admit it) that nobody else can do these things as well as you can? Maybe you think delegating needs to be to a staff member or an assistant—one that you don't have, of course. But there are many other kinds.

I am going to give you nine ideas for things you can delegate. Of course they won't all apply to you. It depends on your situation, your stage of motherhood, and what you do. Still, I am willing to bet that there is at least one thing on the list that you *can* delegate, and if you go through with delegating it, you will get back the gift of found time.

NINE THINGS TO DELEGATE

1. Cooking. No, you probably can't hire a cook, but there are a variety of ways you can make cooking easier. Buy precut fruits and veggies instead of doing that step yourself. Or try a service, such as Dream Dinners, where you get the ingredients for several meals that you prep and store in your freezer until you're ready to cook them. Buy cupcakes for your kid's party instead of making them yourself. Or do a meal swap with other moms where you each make multiple servings of one meal and then trade them for others. Cooking and baking take tons of time. If you love it, well by all means, keep doing it. But I bet there is at least one area where you can delegate out some of the time-consuming work.

2. Food Shopping. How much time does your food shopping normally take? For me, my big weekly trip easily takes two hours of time between driving and shopping. If you order online, you can get that down to a quick trip to the market for some fresh essentials. This one is a no-brainer! Totally worth it! You can subscribe to a company, such as Thrive, and pay $59 dollars for a year to have most of your foods delivered. It's like Whole Foods meets Costco. You get great organic, non-GMO food for nearly 50 percent off the average retail price. I also use Amazon Fresh. My groceries are delivered right to my door! Life changing!

3. Driving. We drive and drive as moms. We are truly a taxi service. We drive to school and to sports. Carpool for goodness sakes! Get it organized. Find some other moms and drive a group! You can get your daily driving down to one drive per week if the carpool is big enough! Truly treat your fellow moms like a village. If you are going to Target, find out what your neighbor needs. Help each other out!

4. Cleaning. Now I know some of you are thinking that I'm suggesting luxury items that you can't afford. I totally get it! But think about the value of your time. How long does it take you to clean the whole house? The toilets included? That would take me an entire day. If you didn't spend the day cleaning, could you do something more valuable? Share quality time with your family? Or make more money? You might hire someone to do laundry. My friend started a brilliant company called Laundry Ladies; she does your laundry, folds it, and puts it on your doorstep. It's your call. Only you know what you need. But it may be worth giving up a latte here and there to have your house cleaned for you.

5. Chores. Don't forget to find cleaning that the kids can do. They can start helping out with age-appropriate chores pretty young. My kids take out the trash, do the dishes, and do their own laundry! Kids can help you make dinner. Your kids can pack lunches, too! Create little bins of foods they should choose from to make it easy for them to pack a well-balanced lunch. Kids can vacuum and sweep. Yes, kids can even clean bathrooms. Create a chore chart (page 220). I know most of us give up on this because kids don't do a good enough job or we have to nag them. That's a training issue, people. God, I sounded just like my husband there. Do the chore with them several times. Create a habit, and stick with it until it becomes second nature. Any help you can get is work that you don't have to do.

6. Volunteering. I know in the past that I felt like I should volunteer in my kid's classroom or on the school field trip. If this is difficult for you, come up with a plan. My husband and I decided that he volunteers for school field trips and I volunteer in the class. I usually volunteer to be the art-mom because it is less time intensive than being a weekly helper. If the school doesn't advertise a position as a shared position, let the teacher know that you're happy to help if you can share the work with another parent. This year I'm sharing art-mom duties with two other parents. I get the joy of helping in my daughter's class, but I only have to commit to being art-mom every other month.

7. Family Support. Sit down with your partner and talk about all the things you do every day. Bring a list. You do a lot! Ask if there is anything that your partner might be able to help with. My husband, for example, does all of the laundry. Maybe your partner could help by running an errand on the way home from work, taking your car in for service, or dropping off clothes at the cleaner. It all helps. If you ask nicely, I bet you will get a yes. You can also ask other family members to help you once or twice a week with the kids. If you are lucky enough to have grandparents on the scene, they would probably feel honored to have some private time with the kids.

8. Virtual Assistance. If you are a working mom, you have got to check out Fiverr and Elance. These sites offer virtual assistants who do everything from social media and podcast editing to graphic design and bookkeeping. There's a site called Fancy Hands (fancyhands.com) where you can hire virtual assistants to do anything from planning your vacation to ordering your holiday cards. If hiring virtual help is of interest to you, I highly recommend that you also check out Chris Ducker's book and program *Virtual Freedom: How to Work with Virtual Staff to Buy More Time, Become More Productive, and Build Your Dream Business.*

9. Online Shopping. One last way to delegate is to shop online whenever you can. I rarely go out shopping because it takes too much time! Get Amazon Prime, and get everything from your dog food to your makeup delivered. Don't have time to hunt through big department stores for a new outfit? There are now subscription services for clothes. Seriously, Le Tote is like Netflix for clothing. Stitch Fix is another popular one. It's like having a personal shopper, but you never have to go to the store.

The ultimate thing you need to do to manage your time better is to stop trying to be super mom. Let go of the guilt. Let go of feeling inadequate. We are not martyrs. We will be better wives, mothers, and people in general if we can get ourselves out of being overwhelmed.

Don't worry if things aren't done just right or your way. Stop being the whirling dervish spinning doing ten tasks at a time. Yes, we know you can do it. But there are people around you, called your family, who can help. Take that help and you will be given the ultimate gift—a little bit of time. And it's up to you to make sure you don't just fill it right back up again. A good mother is not the one who gets the most done. To be a truly great leader in your family, you need to slow down and be purposeful with your time.

I'm not sure who said it, but I'll share it again: You can do anything, but you can't do everything.

Counterbalance

We are living in a fight-or-flight world. This reaction was fine in the cave days when we encountered a saber-toothed tiger. Our adrenaline pumped. Our heart rates increased. Our blood went to our extremities so we could run. Then we got to rest when we were safely back in our caves. The problem is that we aren't resting anymore. We are just living in a high-stress, chaotic routine.

We all know we should balance this stress with calming downtime. But is that balance really possible? I've talked about using yes and no as ways to balance your life. We should also consider an additional perspective: one of counterbalance instead of just balance. No matter how much you plan, there will be times when motherhood will take over and other times when work or life will dominate. Times of imbalance may be seasonal or change by the day. Our tendency is to tilt out of balance, so let's focus on counterbalance, on cramming our life with what we love most. Appealing, isn't it?

The beauty of counterbalance is that you can achieve it by giving the neglected things more time. If you have had a long work week, balance it out by spending extra quality time with your family on the weekend. If you have spent most of the day trying to discipline your child, take the early evening time to let go and have a family playtime where the only requirement is to have fun. Stress comes in when you continue to burn the candle at both ends and you neglect the need to bring things back into balance.

On your Wheel of Life, you identified where you are out of balance. Try to pay attention to the times when you clearly feel out of balance, and then give yourself a counterbalance. But you need more time for that, you say? I agree. You've learned how to prioritize your MITs, prune away things that aren't worth your time, and delegate tasks to save you time. Let's talk next about how to make more time.

Parkinson's Law

Have you heard of Parkinson's Law? I bet you've at least experienced it. It means that work expands to fill the time available for completion. In other words, we give tasks more time than they really need.

Remember when you had all semester to study for an exam, but you crammed it into twenty-four hours? Or you had all month to make your son's Halloween costume, but did it all the night before? Or maybe you worked on a project for three months, but it could have been done in two days?

Why does this matter? Moms feel like they don't have enough time. If I can help you defeat Parkinson's Law, that means I've helped you find some time. The basic solution is this: If work expands to the time allotted, give yourself less time. Basically, you need to create artificial time constraints for yourself and see what happens. Here are three ways to try this.

HOW TO DEFEAT PARKINSON'S LAW

1. Take a task, such as doing the laundry, and give yourself half the amount of time to get it done. For instance, if you normally fold laundry for half an hour, try to get it done in fifteen minutes. I think you'll be surprised at the results.

2. Put time limits on things that sap your time, such as Facebook or email. Set a timer, then get in, do your thing, and get out.

3. If there is something you don't want to do, get it done first! The satisfaction of getting those things out of the way will speed you through the rest of the day.

When you learn how to set the right time constraints for yourself, you will have more freedom. Now, be careful not to mindlessly fill that time up with more unnecessary tasks. Choose carefully what you will do with

MAKE MORE TIME

more time—exercise, meditate, spend time in nature, or anything else that serves your MITs—because now you will be able to do it!

Our time is finite. Don't just fill your hours. Fill them with what you love, including recharge time. Do this and I can assure you that you will get to enjoy a little bit of that balance we all crave.

Mommy Hack: How to Save Ten Minutes Every Day

How would you like to have an extra sixty hours in a year to do whatever you want? The possibility almost makes you cry, doesn't it? Well, get out your tissues, because this is absolutely possible. All it takes is ten minutes saved per day . . . and I've already created a list of ideas to help you to make this happen.

TEN WAYS TO SAVE TEN MINUTES REPEATEDLY

1. Make a daily list for your kids. Even before my kids could read, I had a checklist with pictures so they knew what they needed to have done before school or to get ready for a sport. Examples include shoes on, backpack, homework, lunch. Laminate the list and they can check it off each day.

2. Wash and cut all of your produce one time per week. Use a product like Eat Cleaner and the produce will last longer. Not only will you eat healthier, you'll also save time by avoiding the clean-cut-pack-cleanup process multiple times during the week.

3. Have handy baskets around the house for items that you regularly use. For new moms, I'm talking about things such as wipes and diapers. For any of us, maybe pens, hair ties, reading glasses, small notepads, and sticky notes.

4. Take one, give one. If your child gets a new toy or article of clothing, have him pick one of his own to give away to someone in need. Not only does this teach your child the gift of giving, it helps keep your home from getting cluttered and saves you cleaning time. Bonus!

5. Get your exercise in when your kids are at lessons or sports. I understand that you want to watch your kids. But, truth be told, I see more moms on their phones the whole time than actually watching their kids' activities. This is a great time to get a little valuable time in for you!

6. Have kids be ready ten minutes earlier than they need to be. No TV, video games, or dawdling until they are 100 percent ready to go. Teaching them to be ready early is a great life skill to keep them from developing the habit of running late.

7. Buy your kids the same type of socks in bulk. That way you never have to work to find a match because they all match!

8. Put lunch foods in separate bins to make it easy for your kids to pack their own lunches. For instance, bars in one bin, fruit snacks in another, chips or pretzels in another. Let your kids know how many items to pick from each bin. They can start packing their own lunches earlier than you think!

9. Have a shared digital calendar with your spouse or other caretaker(s)—and include your kids when they are old enough. Putting all sports, play dates, birthday parties, and other activities on the same digital calendar allows every caretaker to know who is available, what is coming up, and how to get there. That way you don't spend extra time trying coordinate.

10. Double up. At least once a week, double the amount of what you're making for dinner and put the extra portions in the freezer. This builds up your arsenal of frozen meals for busy nights.

Remember what I said earlier about how we all have the same twenty-four hours in a day? And that the difference in how you experience that time is in how you choose to use those twenty-four hours?

To help you make those choices, I put together some tips that have helped me make the most of my time.

Nine Practical Ways to Make the Most of Your Precious Time

1. Budget your time. Many of us use a budget for our finances. Although your plan doesn't always match reality, a well-planned budget guides your spending and helps keep you from overspending. What if you also had a budget for your time? It might even be more important than a budget for your finances.

This time-budget concept comes from one of my virtual mentors, Michael Hyatt. He calls the time-budget his Ideal Week, and it has been a game changer for me. (You can find a URL for his article and budget template on page 220.) Most of us just react to our day, tackling either what has to get done or what is right in front of us. Then we repeat that same "method" day after day. No wonder we end up exhausted and overwhelmed!

What if you planned your days around themes that focus on what's truly important to you and your family? That's the main idea of Michael Hyatt's Ideal Week: budgeting your time according to themes. I encourage you to try it!

+ Choose your tool. Either a spreadsheet or a digital calendar will work. I used my Google calendar.
+ Create your themes.
+ Plan your week around your themes.

For instance, I plan certain days for meetings and center other days on writing or projects. You could also break up your day around your MITs. Block out some time for exercise, meditation, or prayer. Block out some time for family and some time for business. Schedule some time for sharpening your saw, as Stephen Covey says.

Give me six hours to chop down a tree and
I will spend the first four sharpening the axe.

—ABRAHAM LINCOLN

Most importantly, have a plan, and let it guide you.

2. Create margin. This one is so important I'll say it again: create margin. Most of us book our day completely full, packing every minute so tightly that we barely have time to breathe. This is why we are always so overwhelmed. Think about the margin in this book. If we didn't have it, the words would spread to the edges of the paper. We need margin.

The antidote, then, is to plan your schedule so you have some space. You need to have time to pee, for one thing! Give yourself what might seem like "extra" time, breathing room for when meetings run long or something doesn't go as planned—because that happens all the time, right? Schedule in some "nothing" time. Seriously . . . block out a small (or large) chunk of time and label it "Nothing." Giving yourself planned breaks gives your mind a break. It gives you a moment to recharge. How nice would it be to not be rushed, to let go of that stress of overbooking and constant racing? Do it. Starting now.

3. Say no. We've already talked about this, but I want to make sure you remember that every time you say yes you are in effect saying no to something else. Your hours are already filled to the max. So when you add something on, you always remove the room for something else, right? Unfortunately, that's not usually how we do it. We live under the illusion that we can somehow gut it out and do more, but we must stop that kind of thinking. What can—and will—you say no to? What are you doing that is not serving your MITs? What could be done by someone else? Say yes to what is truly important to you, and say no to everything else.

4. Do one thing at a time. We all have the same 168 hours in the week, but we each get to choose how we use those hours. Most of us think the solution is to multitask and get a bunch of things done at once, but that's actually ineffective and inefficient. There is no good multitasking. In fact, our brains can only focus on one task at a time. When we "multitask" we are actually just switching our attention between tasks very quickly. True, moms can switch their attention on a dime, but at what cost? None of the tasks get full attention, and our brains get worn out with the constant switching. In the worst-case scenarios, this inattention could be life-threatening (texting while driving, for example).

Instead, choose one thing to work on at a time. When writing this list, for example, I shut down my email, Facebook, and Skype. I freed myself from distractions so I could focus. Remember, pilots and surgeons do not multitask when doing their jobs. Neither should you!

Still not convinced multitasking is inefficient? A study done in 2005 showed that multitasking lowers your IQ more than smoking pot does. No, I'm not suggesting you smoke pot! I am suggesting, however, that you choose one task at a time to work on.

5. Batch your tasks. Every time you pick up your phone to check a text, Facebook, or email while you are doing something else is stressing your brain. Instead, try batching similar tasks together into a specific part of the day.

- email
- social media
- phone calls
- going through mail
- spending time with family
- cooking

While nothing can truly be multitasked, it's also not a bad idea to do *mindless* tasks at the same time. For instance, you can listen to a podcast while folding laundry or emptying the dishwasher, because those physical tasks are so familiar to you. But if you try to check email while being with your daughter, then you will not be fully present in either area. Chances are that your daughter and your email recipient will be well aware of that.

6. Compile one list. This is a takeaway from David Allen's Getting Things Done program. Many of us have about ten million lists written on sticky notes, legal pads, paper scraps, apps, and computer programs. Handy in the moment, these scattered lists quickly become a waste of valuable time, proving to be inefficient and overwhelming. The solution? Choose one single tool for your master list.

As much as I like pen to paper, I think the wise choice today is a virtual list that is accessible on your phone and computer. With so many great apps out there, it doesn't matter which one you choose, only that you do choose one. (See page 220 for suggestions.) Write down (or type) everything in that one tool: from going to the cleaners to signing your son up for pre-school to taking a break for YOU.

David Allen suggests that you break up that single list into segments so that you are batching same types of items. For example, computer tasks in one grouping, home tasks in another grouping, and out-of-the-house tasks in yet another grouping. This way you aren't distracted by looking at "Pick up dry cleaning" when you are sitting in front of your computer.

7. Reflect and plan. Schedule one of the last blocks of your day for reflection and planning. How did your day go? What did you get done? What didn't you get done? What would you like to get done tomorrow? Ideally, write down your three MITs for the next day and set them out so you can start your day clear and ready. Speaking of clear, also use this time to straighten your desk and create a tidy space for your next day.

8. Put a timer on. Remember Parkinson's Law? You will use the time given. So give yourself realistic, but small, amounts of time to get projects done. A timer will help keep you on track.

9. Track everything important to you. I believe that which gets measured gets done—or at least improved. Most people tend to be fuzzy about what they want and even fuzzier about the plan to get there. I have learned to track anything where I want to see progress. For years now, I have kept little graph-paper journals where I track a variety of health and fitness goals. Each day, I use that journal to track everything from the number of push-ups that I do to the number of glasses of water I drink. I also track my moods and my periods. In that last case, I'm not trying to improve anything; I am building an awareness about how my cycle may affect my mood or my eating choices.

What I track depends on the season of my life and my top-priority goals. Be open to adding and removing things to track as it feels right to you. You might want to track your food, your fitness, your "no" versus "yes" choices, or maybe steps to achieving a goal. For example, right now, I am tracking if I write for eleven minutes a day to get this book done. That's right, I'm writing a book by spending only eleven minutes a day on it. What can you do with eleven minutes over a stretch of time?

March:

**Write down your three MITs each day.
Commit to them before anything else.**

*Stop striving for perfection. Strive to be better than you were yesterday.
Don't just go through this year. Grow through it!*

Chapter 4
Change Your Habits

We've talked about how to become more aware of and intentional with our time by making smart choices. But what if I told you there are also ways that you can save time and energy *without even thinking about it*? This magic tool is called a *habit*—an action or routine that becomes so familiar to you that you do it automatically. In this chapter, I'll help you get started with powerful, positive new habits.

Create Positive Change

In chapter 2 you identified specific goals you want to reach in different areas of your life. I'll teach you a handy way to accomplish goals: creating habits. I won't unroll my whole master's degree in psychology here, but I will touch on the way our thoughts and behaviors work together, and how we can use that to our advantage.

What's your reaction when you hear someone say "go big or go home"? If you're overwhelmed (and we moms often are), you probably figure you might as well "go home" because "going big" is more than you can handle. Well, I have good news for you: There is a different way to look at reaching your big goals, and it is definitely something you can handle.

The Kaizen Approach

Kaizen is a Japanese term created from the words *kai*, meaning change, and *zen*, meaning good. Combined, they mean change for the better. A key feature of kaizen is that big results come from many small changes that build up over time: consistent incremental improvement by everyone involved. To get a better idea of the spirit of kaizen, consider the ocean. We think of the ocean as one huge thing, but the ocean is made up of zillions of drops of water. Whatever big thing you want to accomplish can in fact be thought of many small parts. (For additional details, check kaizen.com.)

You can apply this kaizen approach to create healthy and helpful habits in any part of your life—from parenting to business to learning to fitness.

Kaizen Exercise

Take a look back at the dream life you described in chapter 2.

What would you like to achieve?

_____

_____

What would be the first step you would take to get there?

_____

_____

What small step would follow that?

_____

_____

This is how you make big dreams come true. Small steps. One after another. Building progress and getting you closer to the goal!

Do any of these steps overwhelm you? Then they are still too big. Break them down into something smaller.

You don't have to have every step figured out. Just take the next step. And then the next day, take the next step.

This, my friends, is how I live my whole life. The baby step concept has appealed to me for a long time. As a child, I was easily overwhelmed. I was never a natural in anything: sports, friends, you name it. I didn't believe I could do anything successfully, and I just stopped trying. Later in life, I realized my approach needed to change, so I started breaking things down to the smallest achievable bite.

When I decided to run my first marathon, the distance of 26.2 miles was overwhelming. I sat down with a calculator and piece of paper. How far could I currently run? What small increase could I handle each week? How long would it take to get to 26.2 at that rate? That's how long I needed to get ready for my marathon. And it worked!

Working in these small steps gets me through every major goal—even writing this book! You will find that with most things you will build more stamina and be able to make bigger steps as you proceed on any journey.

Create New Habits

When we talk about incremental steps and the kaizen approach, what we're really talking about is building new habits. A great example of this comes from Stanford researcher B.J. Fogg, who explored habit formation by focusing on how to get people to floss their teeth. He instructed people to floss one tooth after they brushed their teeth. That step of flossing just one tooth was so small, so doable, that they agreed to commit to that small task. Before long, they built a habit of flossing one tooth and that soon grew to a habit of flossing two teeth, then three, and eventually all of their teeth. Fogg suggests you build up a baby step at a time. If, for instance, you want to meditate for twenty minutes per day, then start with one minute. The following week make it two minutes. And so forth. (For more about Fogg's research, go to bjfogg.com.)

When I don't feel like working out, I commit to working out for just ten minutes. Once I get started, my mind-set changes and I am encouraged to keep going.

If we give ourselves a task so small that it seems almost ridiculous, we will succeed in doing it. Each tiny success gives us a little boost and that motivates us to repeat our success. Next thing we know, we've added another task and we've succeeded there, too. Those successes add up much more than you might expect.

Researchers believe this works is because we have a dissonance with starting something new. It seems so hard, so overwhelming to add something to our repertoire of habits, and our brain seems to resist getting started. The more boring, frustrating, or hard the task seems, the more likely we are to procrastinate. Psychologists have found that you are more likely to get stared if you break a task down so it doesn't seem so negative.

So, just get started, because humans have an instinctive drive to finish a task once they've begun it. I guess the cliché about the first step being the hardest is true. If your kids don't want to do their homework (I speak from personal experience), just sit them down and get started. It won't be so hard to move forward once you begin!

If you are trying to change the way you eat, develop your fitness, or help your child make some changes, consider the kaizen approach. For eating, change one snack each day to a healthier one. Then, over time, add those small changes to mealtime. For fitness, choose one exercise to start with. Or, if you want to improve your regiment, focus on getting in one just more rep or one more interval of time for each workout. To help your children make changes, have them choose one tiny thing they can change to get them closer to the desired behavior. Then add on from there. Baby steps add up.

Compound Interest

If you like this concept of small changes having a significant effect over time, you should read *The Slight Edge* by Jeff Olson. The basic idea is that at any time, you are making very small, seemingly inconsequential decisions that are either making your life better or worse. There is no standing still; that path of small decisions—the slight edge—is either working for you or against you.

Take, for example, compound interest. Olson shares a story where you are offered either one million dollars right now, or a penny per day, doubled each day, for one month. Which would you choose? Unless you've read this illustration before, you'll probably choose the right-now million dollars. It seems to make sense, but you would be making the wrong choice (assuming, of course, that your goal was to end up with more money). One penny, doubled every day for a month adds up to $10,737,418 . . . and 24 cents. It's hard to believe but I've done the math to confirm it! Compare that to $1,000,000, and you see that compound interest wins.

Where might compound interest be adding up in your life? Is your weight higher than is healthy? It wasn't just one giant meal that made you overweight. Has your physical fitness faded away? It wasn't just one day of missed exercise that got you out of shape. It is the culmination of small choices made every single day that contribute to problems like obesity, high cholesterol, and diabetes.

The good news is that the way you got in (the small choices) is the way you also get out. Those small choices can work in your favor quite powerfully. Stop trying to make a dramatic change; just make a slightly better choice than you did yesterday. Every time you have a decision to make, ask yourself how you can better it by one degree. Just one.

The key here is to make a plan and stay consistent. Decide what small step you will take each day, what different choice you will make, then plan how you will make that happen. You don't have to be perfect to gain traction. If you stay focused on your goal and stay positive, your brain functions more smoothly, and then the changes happen more easily. You. Can. Do. This.

Don't Break the Chain

One way to motivate yourself is to create a "chain" of success that you won't want to break. Jerry Seinfeld was once asked how he had so many jokes, and his answer was that he had committed to writing jokes every single day. He pulled out a giant calendar and marked a big red X for every day that he wrote, sticking to his one goal of not breaking the chain. Once you decide something you want to work on, commit to it like Jerry did.

Be careful, though, not to commit to too much, or you will probably give up. Just pick one truly important thing and work on it a little bit, in some tiny way, every day. For example, while writing this book, my goal was to write eleven minutes every single day. Although I missed plenty of days, the more days I was able to write consecutively, the more momentum I picked up . . . and you now have my eleven minutes per day in your hands. Small steps add up!

For instance, if you want to run a marathon but currently don't run, then start to run at least a little bit each day. If you want to take a trip around the world, spend ten minutes per day researching what your next step would be. If you want a better marriage, spend five minutes a day putting energy to your love life. No matter how big or small, the most successful people are the most consistent!

Can you track everything from food to fitness, business to parenting? You could. But I wouldn't recommend it. In business, we track KPIs (key performance indicators). Think of the dashboard of your car. It measures maybe four key things (gas, oil, temperature, speed). I really know nothing about cars, but I'm guessing it could measure twenty other things. That would be too overwhelming. So, they give you the four most important things.

What are the key performance indicators for your healthy and happy life? I am a crazy measurer. I have notebooks upon notebooks for tracking my personal life. It changes depending on the season of my life. Focus on what's most important to you and then don't break the chain!

Seasons of Your Life

One other important thing to take into consideration is that everything has a season. There is a time, a season, for everything, and habits that serve you well this season might stop being helpful in a different season. Think about nature. Spring is the time for new birth, new growth. Fall reminds us that everything has a beginning and an end. Winter is a time to hibernate. If you feel as though you need different habits for different seasons, by all means go for it. Don't keep a habit that no longer serves you!

Positive Change Exercise

While this topic is fresh in your mind, let's go ahead and take action on it.

What is one current habit you are not happy with?

_____

_____

_____

What is one new positive habit that could replace the habit you wrote about above?

_____

_____

_____

What are the first three baby steps you will take to create that new habit and ditch the old one?

1. _____

2. _____

3. _____

Note: If your new habit is about fitness, check out the link to the baby-step workout template on page 158.

Maximizing Good Habits—
A Morning Ritual for Mom

One way to take advantage of habits is to put them together into a routine, something you do each day to boost your day without draining your energy. Let's talk about mornings. Mornings can be rough, especially if you are a mom to school-aged children.

There are tantrums about getting out of bed and getting dressed. There is chaos over what to eat for breakfast or pack for lunch. And there is never enough time before you are rushing out the door. There is no easing into the day. Ugh! I cringe at the stressful mornings that were a part of my past. I think of the meme that I started the day feeling like Mary Poppins and sent them off to school sounding like Darth Vader. I wasn't happy with kicking off my day like this and realized that something needed to change.

In this case, it's your morning routine. Please, please, please rethink your days and put a morning routine in there! It doesn't need to be a long, drawn-out routine, but it does need to be meaningful, intentional, and consistent. (There's that word again.)

Moms often feel like they have no control over their day, with no time for themselves. Committing to a healthy morning routine can give you back your control and help you restore some of that much-needed life balance. A morning routine sets the tone for your day, motivating you and filling you with the energy you will need for later hours. Also, when you start the day with a healthy morning routine, you are more likely to make healthy choices throughout the day. Remember the compound interest we just talked about? With a morning routine, you start making those small, right choices as soon as you wake up. And, when it truly becomes a routine, you barely need to think about the choices; they become second nature.

It's no coincidence that many successful people credit their morning routine for their results. Jane Austin, Marilyn Monroe, and Audrey Hepburn all swore by their morning routines. Modern mamas such as Kim Kardashian, Jennifer Lopez, and Gwyneth Paltrow—to name a few—have shared how their morning rituals set them up for success in the day. Oprah swears by her morning ritual of meditation. Arianna Huffington starts every day with yoga. You, too, can have a morning ritual that will set you up for success.

Five Tips for Setting Up
Your Mommy Morning Routine

I know it can be overwhelming to think of yet another something to add to your day. Remember to think of the routine as collecting the good habits you want to employ throughout the day. It's about blocking your time in a super beneficial way. Trust me, this is a gift for you! You will begin to look forward to your mornings if they become a special time for you.

If you have babies and toddlers, a morning routine might not be possible for you yet. You are probably sleep deprived, and you have little control over your morning. Just know all moms empathize with you, and if you can manage ten minutes of "me" time in the morning, it will do you a world of good! If you can't, don't worry. They will be school age before you know it, and you'll get to set up your morning routine then!

Okay, here are a few tips to get you started. Notice that none of these tips require much time, and none of them are huge steps. They will set you up beautifully to create a new positive habit and incremental positive change.

1. Wake up earlier. I know you don't want to hear this, so let's just get it over with as the first tip. You will rarely find a successful person who doesn't get up early. I'm not making this up. (Sorry!) People who get up early tend to be happier, live longer, be more productive, and make more money. The simple truth is that you can't fit anything else in your day if you don't get up a little earlier. Start with ten minutes, then increase from there as you're able.

I don't, however, want you to sacrifice sleep, so you might need to give up that episode of *The Bachelor* or *Scandal* and set your alarm for ten minutes earlier. And you definitely need to change your paradigm: Instead of saying "I'm not a morning person," tell yourself "this is my special time." It's okay if you don't become a "morning person" who bounces out of bed joyfully every morning. As one of my friends says, "I don't like *getting up* early, but I love *being up* early." What matters is that you get up and do your routine. It will change your life.

2. Create a ritual. Rituals are incredibly comforting. You can count on them each day, knowing they are like a best friend who always supports you. Start your day with a cup of coffee or tea before anyone else is up. *Do not* check your phone or computer, even if you think it will help you ease into your day. Facebook is a little like playing Russian roulette because you never know what information and moods people will put out there. Facebook should not drive your day; you should! That's the whole point of this morning routine. Consider journaling, reading, or meditating. Many find this early morning quiet time to be a wonderful space for prayer or inspirational reading. Or get yourself a set of good colored pencils and one of the adult coloring books that are so hot right now and color your way into the morning. Experiment and see what you're most drawn to, then make that part of your routine.

3. Exercise. Consider starting your day with movement. If you can get your exercise done before your family wakes up, you are golden for the day! Try an early morning Body Back class if it's available near you, or if you have stroller-age kids, go to Stroller Strides with your little cherub. Exercise in the morning will pump up your energy and your endorphins, giving you a much more positive perspective for your day. If you get your exercise over with early, you won't have the rest of the day to come up with an excuse for skipping it. You know what I'm talking about. I am someone who LOVES to exercise. But if I don't get it in first thing in the morning, even I will make up 100 excuses to skip it later in the day.

4. Write down your three MITs. The morning can also be a great time of productivity. Take a look at your calendar for the day and decide the three most important things you need to get done that day. Write them down, including when you will do them that day. This puts you in the driver's seat for your day before it drives you. This gives you CONTROL. That sounds amazing, doesn't it? Commit to this, and you will put yourself in charge.

5. Pre-prep. This is a suggestion for the evening before, but it still affects your morning. Pre-prep lunches, lay out the next day's clothes for your kids (and yourself), sign homework, and pack backpacks at night. You can even pre-prep breakfast. Then take a look at tomorrow's schedule so you are clear on what you want to accomplish the following day. The goal is to get as much ready as you can the night before so you have a smoother morning. Even if you are tired in the evening, this pre-prep is well worth sticking it out for just a few more minutes before stopping for the evening!

Mommy Morning Routine Exercise

Take ten minutes (yes, you can find ten minutes) to write down things you would love to do in your morning routine, even if doing all of them would take way too much time.

_____

_____

_____

_____

_____

_____

_____

Out of all the possibilities you wrote down, list your top three choices.

_____

_____

_____

Look at how much time each of your top choices will take. Now decide which one or ones you can realistically do each morning.

How much earlier will you get up tomorrow morning to do this? (Yes, I said tomorrow. We're starting this right now!)

Congratulations! You have a plan! Try this out for a few days, and note what works and doesn't work. Make adjustments as necessary. You will know when you have *your* right routine.

There is one more part of this topic concerning morning routines that we need to discuss. Setting up your morning routine might be challenging, but the most difficult part might be *protecting* that routine. You must decide that your morning routine is nonnegotiable (except, of course, for emergencies), or I can guarantee you that you will slip away from your routine.

Consider your morning routine to be absolutely sacred. Commit to it yourself, then let your family know your morning routine is your time and they must honor it. It might sound selfish, but it's actually self-ish (review chapter 1 for a refresher). It will make everyone's day go much better. It will set up the day's momentum and make you feel unstoppable—and that makes for a much happier mom. And we all know a happy mom means a happier family, right?

The most important thing here is to set the tone for your day before someone else does it for you. Take control. This day is yours.

Meditation

Some of you might have already chosen meditation as part of your morning routine, because it's one habit we are, surprisingly, hearing a lot about in the media these days. But I have to admit something to you. I have had the opportunity to train thousands of women over the course of my career. I have gotten people to change their exercise habits and their nutrition habits and their work habits, but creating this new habit of meditation for myself has been a huge challenge. I've failed at it many times. If you roll your eyes when you hear about meditation, I definitely understand! The idea of sitting and doing nothing when you have so much to do is, well, it's just absolutely crazy. Also, for most of us, sitting quietly doing nothing—probably in the midst of chaos—when there is so much to do is anything but relaxing.

But this isn't helping you want to start meditating, is it? What if I tell you that I have been inconsistently meditating for nearly twenty years, but I have *finally* been consistent with daily meditation for the last five of those years? That is true, and it has absolutely changed my life.

HOW I GOT STARTED

I stumbled into meditation when I was taking yoga classes from a friend and mentor, Michele Hébert. I was going to be her guest at Rancho La Puerta, a beautiful resort near San Diego, California, so she was going to pick me up and we would go together to the resort. I accidentally messed up the directions to my house, so she arrived stressed-out after getting all turned around and caught in traffic. This was before GPS and before cell phones, so she couldn't easily call me for additional guidance. I had never seen my calm, spiritual friend so flustered. Apparently she actually was human.

Still stressed as we arrived at the ranch, Michele took me to a special meditation room so she could decompress and regain her calm spirit. We took a seated meditation pose. And we sat. And sat. And sat. It was so very painful for me, nothing relaxing about it. *How long is she going to sit like that?* I wondered. *How long are we going to be here? My hips are killing me. Can I move? Or will that mess her up?* I'm pretty sure as she got more and more relaxed, I got more and more stressed.

Afterward, when I expressed my discontent to Michele, she explained that meditation is a practice and that means you have to, well, *practice.* Maybe you start with one minute, then the next time two minutes, and so on (again with the incremental changes), and eventually you will be meditating for long chunks of time, willingly.

WHY MEDITATE?

So, if meditation is so difficult, why would we want to do the work of making it a habit?

Think about getting a massage. You know that feeling you get when you are somewhere between awake and asleep—and it's nothing short of delicious?

Meditation can help you bring on that feeling, without a massage, and that is honestly about enough of a reason for me. But I'll give you more reasons to meditate, and these are not some new age, hippy dippy ideas. They are all scientifically proven. From studies done at Harvard to work being done at Center for Pain Medicine at Emory Healthcare in Atlanta, Georgia, Western medicine and institutions have been proving the positive effects of meditation for decades.

SIX SCIENTIFIC BENEFITS OF MEDITATION

1. It increases happiness. We can all use more of that.

2. It strengthens your immune system. The last thing we need is to get sick. Meditation is like pre-healing.

3. It decreases stress. Many women come to me as stressed-out moms, and many of them complain about stress eating. Meditation is a powerful way to decrease that stress and related bad habits.

4. It improves your memory, attention, and focus. In other words, meditation strengthens your brain.

5. It benefits your body in ways we don't totally understand. Positive effects include helping to counteract heart disease, osteoporosis, sleep problems, digestive problems, depression, and obesity.

6. It is good for our relationships. Couples say that they become more loving when they meditate. (No, I have not gotten my husband to meditate; I'm just sharing the scientific facts.)

If you are concerned about having to figure out and learn the right way to meditate, with the right equipment, facing the right direction, during the right time of the day, drop all of those concerns right now. Simply sit quietly. That's all you need to learn or do. You have probably heard that the goal of meditation is to have no thoughts, but that will basically never happen. A mind never turns off. However, the chatter of thoughts does quiet down . . . with practice. As you begin to experiment with meditation, try some of these ways to help quiet your mind chatter:

> Focus on your breath.
> Focus on a word or mantra.
> Focus on a sound.
> Focus on a mental image of someone you love deeply,
>   then focus on that feeling.

The act of bringing the mind back to the focus (your breath, a word, etc.) *is* the meditation. When your mind wanders, that's not a failure, it's simply part of the practice. In fact, that practice of coming back to the focus is what you carry with you through the whole day. You will naturally start to come back to your breathing when you are at wit's end with your child, or you will suddenly remember your focus word when you're about ready to shout at a family member or have a meltdown. Meditation is wonderful during the sitting quiet time, but an equally powerful benefit is the way it changes your reactions in the rest of your daily life.

I am certain that my days are much better when I meditate, and I feel more grounded and calmer. On the days that I don't meditate, I am more agitated, quicker to yell, and definitely feel (and show) more stress. The bottom line is that I respond better to the chaos of family life when I meditate in the morning. This is a habit that has had a profound effect on my peace and happiness. It might be one for you to consider, too!

A MORNING ROUTINE WITH
MEDITATION PRACTICE EXAMPLE

My morning meditation practice starts with waking up before the rest of my family does. I take about ten minutes to write in my journal, then I read a passage or quote from an inspirational book. (I'm currently reading *Wide Awake. Every Day. Daily Inspiration for Conscious Living* by my friend Starla J. King.) I then put on some soft nature music or meditation music from iTunes or Spotify, set a timer for eleven minutes—just because eleven is my favorite number—and sit. I sit upright on a couch with a pillow in my lap that my arms rest on. I sit crisscross applesauce (boy am I a mom!), but you can sit with your feet on the floor if you are more comfortable. My eyes are closed, unless my meditation has me gazing at a candle. When the timer goes off, I take a deep breath in and out, then stand up to start the rest of my day. That's it!

After practicing for so long, my mind usually goes into that relaxed space quite quickly. Some days it doesn't, and that's fine; I still benefit from keeping up the practice that day. Some days I feel I need to meditate again later in the day. If I'm feeling particularly stressed or anxious, I tell the kids that mommy needs a time-out, then I go meditate for a few minutes. An unexpected side-effect is that my daughter has gotten curious about my meditating and sometimes she joins me! Actually, both kids have joined me before. They particularly like the meditation where I sit in front of a candle and try to still the flame by being very quiet on the outside and the inside. Rachel also loves the rainbow breath meditation that I do, and she even asks for it sometimes before going to bed.

RAINBOW MEDITATION

Sit in a comfortable position. Allow your eyelids to gently close. Take in a deep breath and now, slowly, allow that breath to drift down through your entire body. Exhale. Take in another deep breath. Let that breath flow down through your chest, your stomach and abdomen, your legs, and all the way down to the soles of your feet.

Using your mind's eye (the imaginary eye between your eyebrows), watch your breath as it flows down your body. Send your breath to the base of your spine and let it light up a beautiful red color. A bright, vibrant red. As you continue breathing, draw the color orange into your lower abdomen. Feel it spreading through your lower back, warming your body. As you continue to breathe, bring that focus up a bit more and feel the color yellow as it fills your belly with yellow like the brightest sun. You and your body are in harmony with this color, and you feel your body relax. With this next breath, rise the color to your chest and feel the color green. Green like the greenest grass of the earth, pure and clean.

Feel the love, balance, compassion of the color green. Keep breathing and rise your breath and the color blue to your throat area. Blue as the deepest, purest ocean. Feel the wisdom and balance of the color blue. And finally as you continue your deep breaths, feel the color violet as it radiates out of the crown of your head. This color brings you connection, knowledge, peace. Breathe deeply and fully and connect all of the colors. Red. Orange. Yellow. Green. Blue. Violet. Feel the colors of the rainbow, bringing you energy, life, health, peace.

OTHER MEDITATION OPTIONS

If someone asks how you are and the answer is "Crazy!" "Busy!" "Stressed!" or something along those lines, that's not good. I don't like that answer, and you shouldn't either. Being crazy-busy is not a badge of honor, not something to be proud of and rewarded for. If you are feeling crazy-busy-stressed, then you owe it to yourself and your family to find a way to chill out.

Depending on the season of your life, my morning practice might not work for you. If it is too hard to wake up earlier than your family when you are a sleep-deprived new mom, you might instead meditate while you are nursing or when your baby is napping. Or, if this whole meditation thing is still a no-go for you, then find your own form of meditation.

Maybe it's prayer, knitting, art, or something else that you tap into easily and daily to recharge your spirit and calm your mind. For example, I use my breath as an energizing de-stressor all day long. Let's try it together in the following exercise.

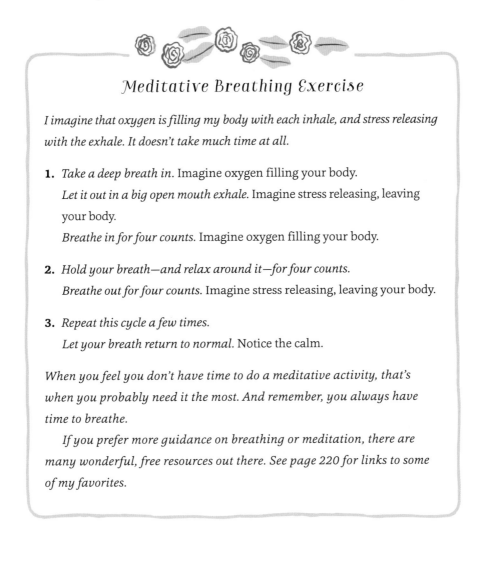

Meditative Breathing Exercise

I imagine that oxygen is filling my body with each inhale, and stress releasing with the exhale. It doesn't take much time at all.

1. *Take a deep breath in.* Imagine oxygen filling your body.
   Let it out in a big open mouth exhale. Imagine stress releasing, leaving your body.
   Breathe in for four counts. Imagine oxygen filling your body.

2. *Hold your breath—and relax around it—for four counts.*
   Breathe out for four counts. Imagine stress releasing, leaving your body.

3. *Repeat this cycle a few times.*
   Let your breath return to normal. Notice the calm.

When you feel you don't have time to do a meditative activity, that's when you probably need it the most. And remember, you always have time to breathe.

If you prefer more guidance on breathing or meditation, there are many wonderful, free resources out there. See page 220 for links to some of my favorites.

April:

**Choose one new habit to focus on this month.
Break it down into baby steps. Commit to making one
small change every day that will help form that habit.**

Stop striving for perfection. Strive to be better than you were yesterday.

Don't just go through this year. Grow through it!

Chapter 5

Change Your Brain, Change Your Life

I know the brain is not technically a muscle, but in my book it is the most important part of your body that you can work out. I have always been fascinated by the wiring of our brains. Think about how often you know what you should do—but you don't do it. Or how you can easily remember something that happened decades ago. Our brains are truly amazing. The best part is that your brain can be trained! In this chapter, I'll show you how.

Mommy Brain

I admit that I have blamed my "mommy brain" for everything from forgetfulness to chaos. It's a nice excuse that can start at pregnancy. If you aren't familiar with mommy brain, it's a real thing. Doctors sometimes call it pregnancy brain. It's that feeling of exhaustion and sluggishness that you feel as a new mom—that feeling of fuzziness and forgetfulness. And, for many of us, it seems like it goes far beyond pregnancy. The good news is our brain is our best place to create a change, and it is strong enough to do so, no matter what stage of motherhood we're in.

Using my background in psychology, I've been trying to figure out why we don't do what we know we should do. Heck, I've been trying to figure out why *I* don't do what I know I should do. We say we want to work out, but we keep pushing the snooze button on our alarm clock and just sleep instead. We say we want to eat healthy foods, but we eat fried chicken. We say we want to accomplish a goal, but we sabotage ourselves. I have looked for years for the secret to actually doing what we want to do. Finally, thanks to all we have learned about the brain in the past five years, I have found that secret. The brain can be trained, just like you can train a muscle!

Our thought patterns have existed for a very long time. If, for example, we give our kids a treat when they are bored, when they are sad, and when they want a reward, they will go through their whole lives thinking that a treat can be the answer to just about everything. Sound familiar? The longer a thought takes a certain path, such as "treats are the answer," the easier it is for it to continue in that direction, so we keep having the same thoughts.

Think you are not worthy?

Think you are not beautiful?

Think you are fat?

Think you are not enough?

How long have you had these thoughts? It's possible they have dug a deep path that your brain keeps following.

We have around 60,000 thoughts per day, and 98 percent of those thoughts are the same thoughts we had yesterday. That means only 2 percent of our thoughts in any given day are new ones! That doesn't mean we can't create many new thoughts each day; it means we just don't bother to intentionally change our thoughts. So why would we want to bother? If your thoughts aren't serving you, then your behaviors probably aren't either. And if your behaviors aren't serving you, the ripple effect is significant.

This beautiful quote from the Upanishads sums it up so well.

Your beliefs become your thoughts,
Your thoughts become your words,
Your words become your actions,
Your actions become your habits,
Your habits become your values,
Your values become your destiny.

So, if you want to change your destiny (or on a smaller scale, your actions), you will need to change your thoughts. The good news is that recent research on neuroplasticity of the brain shows that we can actually change our brains.

Think of a thought as traveling along a trail. The more we repeat that thought, the more it travels the same trail, and that path becomes ingrained. It becomes easy to have that thought because it always knows to go in that direction, down the same trail.

If you want to put a new thought in your head—maybe something a little more empowering—you need to blaze a new trail. Imagine cutting away the branches and making a new path. It's a little bit tough at first, but the more you travel that path, the easier the route. It's the same in your brain. You can create a new path, reminding yourself to travel it often by thinking that same thought, and eventually it will become the "go-to route."

In the book *E²: Nine Do-It-Yourself Energy Experiments That Prove Your Thoughts Create Your Reality*, the author, Pam Grout, suggests that you should consider your 60,000 thoughts a day as prayers. Would you really want to pray for what you are currently thinking about? Would you really pray to not have enough time or to be overwhelmed? It's time to change those prayers (thoughts) to what you actually do want.

When you clean up your thoughts, according to Grout, you clean up the energy that you put out to the world. We need to stop recycling old tapes of knee-jerk conditioning and automatic behaviors that we picked up before we were five years old. How much time are you spending automatically judging, belittling, or second-guessing yourself? Instead, think brilliant ideas that affirm your intentions and create new possibilities.

Think of retraining your thoughts just like you would house-train a puppy. You keep putting the puppy outside until they get what they're supposed to do out there. You don't punish the puppy when it pees in your house, because it doesn't know any better. Instead, you redirect it, placing it outside again. And again. And again. Then one day, the puppy waits, lets you know it needs to go outside, and you realize the learning has finally happened. So now it's time to do the same with your thoughts.

HOW TO HOUSE-TRAIN YOUR THOUGHTS

Think about the puppy-training scenario as you learn how to retrain your own thoughts.

Knowing that we think 98 percent of the same thoughts each day, what negative thoughts enter your head daily?

1. _____
2. _____
3. _____
4. _____
5. _____

How can you change the perspective on that thought? How can you turn that negative into a positive?

1. _____
2. _____
3. _____
4. _____
5. _____

In daily life, use the following steps to retrain your brain:

1. Notice negative thoughts as they come into your head.

2. Gently redirect the negative thoughts, replacing them with new, more positive thoughts.

3. Keep repeating those positive thoughts until your mind starts repeating them back to you.

4. Go out of your way to look for new empowering thoughts to replace the usual 98 percent cycle.

Let me repeat. Your negative thoughts don't serve you. Turn them around. When you can believe that you are worth it, that anything is possible, you will start to see your life turn in an entirely new direction.

THE VOICE INSIDE YOUR HEAD

Let's face it. The voice inside your head does not shut up. It is a never-ending flow of thoughts, a constant chatter that we listen to all day long. I picture that each of us has a gremlin sitting on one shoulder and a goddess sitting on the other. The gremlin tells us all the reasons we can't do something or why we are not good enough. Your gremlin is who drives down your self-confidence and self-worth. The goddess lifts you up, encourages you, and helps you believe in your possibilities. So, who speaks to you more: the gremlin or the goddess?

We do have control over our inner gremlin or goddess. The key is to be aware of your self-talk and redirect it to the positive. We need to learn how to do this ourselves so we can then help our children build their inner goddess or superhero as their beautiful minds are now forging the paths they will take.

THREE WAYS TO REDIRECT YOUR SELF-TALK

1. **Be aware of it.** That's it. Simply noticing that your self-talk is not a positive influence can help you turn it around.

2. **Practice affirmations.** Find a favorite affirmation to repeat daily to create a new pathway in your brain. There are many books and websites that contain great affirmations. See the resources section of this book to get you started.

Here are some examples of powerful affirmations.

1.) I am enough, right here right now.

2.) I am possibility.

3.) I am healthy, happy, and grateful.

4.) I live from love.

5.) My heart is filled with peace and harmony.

6.) I am living the best version of myself.

3. **Surround yourself with the power of positive.** The more you surround yourself with positive people, the more likely you are to feel positive yourself—and vice versa. Surround yourself with positive quotes, podcasts, and messages to influence your positive life.

QUIET THE MOMMY BRAIN

In order to train our brains, we need a little space. That can be quite a challenge in motherhood. Remember when you just wished your baby would say "mommy"? That sweet sound sure feels different after the thousandth time.

Mommy.
Mommy.
Mommy.
Mommy!
Am I right?

Our children don't know about personal space; what's ours is theirs and they are in it! Yes, we know that this time is special, but it also feels a bit like (barely) controlled chaos. So, how can we train our brains in the midst of this chaos? How can we find a small piece of peace where we can have our brains to ourselves, to find the "me" in mommy? I have some tips for you. Some of them will be familiar, so you're already on the way to finding peace!

1. If at all possible, wake up ten minutes before your baby or children wake up. While each minute is precious, ten extra minutes of sleep will not get you out of sleep deprivation. Use those ten minutes to sit with a cup of tea, write in a journal, or meditate. You will be amazed by what happens when you set the tone for your day like this. Hopefully, by now you are already doing this with your new morning routine!

2. Take a four-count breath. There are many moments in your day when you can do some simple breathing exercises. Nursing, driving, dishes. Goodness, do it on the toilet if you need to! Breathe in for four counts, relax around your held breath for four counts, and release for four counts. Mindful breathing has been proven to be calming, energizing, and helpful in reducing stress. My sister teased me when my Apple watch reminded me to breathe. "I already know how to breathe," she said. The unconscious breath to stay alive is quite different than a purposeful breath for peace.

3. Mellow out your music. While it's fun to listen to the latest Lady Gaga hit, it may not be calming those mommy nerves. Consider listening to classical music or sounds of nature. Look up spa music on your favorite online radio program. Music is very powerful and can help reduce stress and create a calming environment. Set the mood to mellow!

4. Scent your stress away. Aromatherapy is one of the fastest growing fields in alternative medicine. Smell is the only sense that can bypass everything (including your thoughts) and go straight to the nervous system. Try any essential oil from lavender to cinnamon, from orange

to lemon balm. Spray it in your car, put it on your wrist in the morning, or douse it on any time your kids are making you melt down.

5. Take a mom-me time-out. Time-outs get a bad rap. Kids think of them as punishment, but really they are a time and place to quiet the brain and regain composure. Moms should consider taking a mom-me time-out regularly (like every day) so they can take a breath, reset, and recharge. My kids have seen me take time-outs for years. Not only is it good for me, they see that I take some space for myself when I need it.

As with all plans, be flexible if they fall through because they do and they will. But keep remembering that your family is at its best when YOU take care of YOU!

Body Image

If you are thinking that you don't have time (there it is again!) to train your brain, that you just need to get things done and can't be bothered with the mental stuff, consider the issues around body image. Notice I didn't say body *type*; I said body *image*—the picture you have *in your mind* of what your body looks like.

You might think that what you tell yourself about your own body is your own business. That it doesn't affect your children or the rest of your family. I don't say this often, but if you believe that you are wrong.

According to the National Eating Disorders Association:
+ Approximately twenty million women suffer from eating disorders
+ Forty-two percent of elementary school students between the first and third grades want to be thinner (Collins, 1991)
+ Eighty percent of ten-year-olds are afraid of being fat (Mellin et al., 1997)
+ Forty-six percent of nine- to eleven-year-olds are "sometimes" or "very often" on diets, and eighty-two percent of their families are "sometimes" or "very often" on diets (Gustafson-Larson & Terry, 1992)

Attitudes toward body image are formed early in life, probably earlier than you ever realized. It's up to us as parents to start our children off with a strong self-image and to combat the pressures from the media. We need to be aware that our own unresolved issues about weight and body image may inadvertently contribute to the pressure on our daughters. The way you speak and act with your own body will have a definite effect on your daughter. *Women don't just decide to hate their bodies. We teach them to.*

One of the reasons for FIT4MOM's popularity nationwide is that moms want to be healthy role models for their children. You might not realize, however, how important your own body image is to your daughter's future. Our talk and behaviors greatly influence our children. Both sons and daughters may experience body image issues and be at risk for eating disorders. We may take for granted how much they take in, even at a young age.

TIPS FOR FORMING A POSITIVE BODY IMAGE

So how can we help our children if we have yet to help ourselves? The answer is we have to start helping ourselves as we help our children. Here are some things you can do to practice healthy body image in your home.

- Keep negative feelings about your own body to yourself, and train your brain to have a more positive view of your body.
- Be proud of your body and all it can do. Focus on function!
- Take compliments when they are given to you.
- Stay away from diets. Let your children see you eat a healthy and balanced selection of foods every day. Time and time again, the clients who tell me that their children are poor eaters are the worst eaters themselves. Your children need to see you eat so they can eat well.
- Model healthy exercise behavior. By taking your kids to Stroller Strides, for example, you are showing your kids that exercise is important to you and that it's fun.
- Don't let your children hear you discussing your weight or dieting. Be very careful about conversations with friends. Your children hear more than you realize!

- Try not to hide your body from your daughter. Be proud of your curves. Being open about your body shows your daughter that you are comfortable and that you have nothing to be ashamed of.
- Choose your television programs and magazines carefully. Images of waif models and extreme makeovers send definite messages to your children about what they should look like.

What we won't do for ourselves, we will do for our children. It's time to start accepting our bodies, if not for our own well-being than for the well-being of our kids.

> *And I said to my body softly, "I want to be your friend." It took a long breath and replied, "I have been waiting my whole life for this."*
>
> —NAYYIRAH WAHEED

From my own page ... My body has been one of my biggest personal battles. I have fought for decades to lose weight and to get fitter, leaner, and more muscular. I have wasted far too much time worrying about my body. It's a vain industry that I work in. When I started working in fitness, I tried every diet. I did everything possible to achieve a certain weight. It was a battle and put me on a never-ending diet cycle. I have now been off that cycle for two decades. And it's been hard. I eat healthy and move almost every day. And I still don't have six pack abs. It's an ongoing struggle for me to say out loud, "I'm healthy and I'm enough, just as I am."

I'm sure that there are some who still judge me for not being lean enough or fit enough as the owner of a fitness company and the creator of a DVD called *Mama Wants Her Body Back*. But I'm hoping that I can be a role model for what real health looks like. Life is just too short to be spent feeling tormented by the body you are in. Even better, I hope that we can love and appreciate our bodies.

Shift Your Focus

Whether it's about body image, negative self-talk, or constant worrying about one thing or another, one specific aspect of training your brain is learning how to shift your focus. What do you see in the picture below?

Take a moment, and look again. Most people tell me they see a circle. But what about the big blue space in the square? Ah, you see it now, don't you? We get what we focus on. And conversely, we also do NOT get what we do NOT focus on.

Think of any optical illusion. You see one picture first, then—because you're looking for it—you shift your focus, and you see the other picture. Maybe that's what we need to do when we look at our lives. Shift our focus and see things differently. In most cases, the life you are living is one you have chosen—and that means you are not a victim.

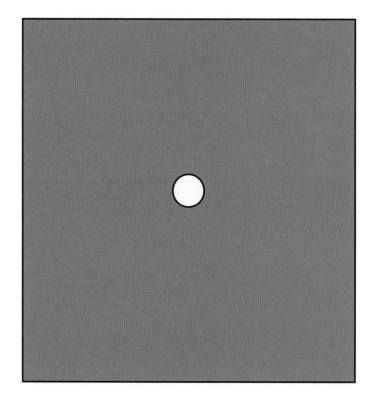

When your toddler is screaming because you won't buy her a toy, shift your focus and smile at the lifelong lesson you are sharing. When you are overwhelmed because you have a hundred emails, think about how lucky you are that so many people want to connect with you. If you want to have more financial freedom, then maybe it's time to give the feeling of abundance more focus.

What is a situation you have had this week that could potentially benefit from a shift of focus?

What was your original response?

Shift your focus. What is a different possibility? What other response might be possible?

The trouble is that most moms are so overwhelmed that they can't figure out how to balance it all. Think back to the previous chapters. What tools have you picked up to help you handle the overwhelm? Your MITs. The words yes and no. Simplifying and pruning. Delegating. Saving ten minutes a day. Changing your habits. Taking baby steps. And now, training your brain. So let's continue.

TURN "CAN'T" INTO "CAN"

Let's use this new "shift your focus" tool to flip your perception on a doozy of a question. How many things do you think you can't do? Write a book? Do a handstand? Bake a soufflé? After decades of living a life of can't, I now believe that there is nothing I can't do. Let me reframe. I think I can do anything if I want to *and* I'm willing to put the work into it. At this moment, I can't bake a soufflé. But I don't really care to. I also can't do a pull-up. That I care to do, so I'm working on it. I am practicing doing pull-ups almost every day, and I know that one day I will be able to do a full pull-up.

Whether you believe you can do a thing
or not, you are right.

—HENRY FORD

Can-Do Exercise

Take a moment, no matter where you are, to think of something you have always wanted to do but never have.

Have you wanted to run a marathon? Start a business? Write a book? Jump out of a plane? Go on a silent retreat? Come on. We all have something. What's yours?

Write down your "Can-Do" activity (even if you don't quite believe it yet):

_____

_____

_____

_____

Reread your "Can-Do" item. What is your brain saying? Is it already piling up obstacles so high you can barely see the "can" anymore for all the "cant's"? Keep reading; I'll help you overcome those obstacles.

OVERCOME

To think that you will get through life without obstacles is unrealistic. I doubt I have to convince you of that! No matter how positive you are, you will encounter rough times. The good news is that you have a choice about how to handle those rough times.

I am convinced that life is 10% what happens to me and 90% how I react to it. And so it is with you. . . we are in charge of our attitudes.

—CHARLES R. SWINDOLL

Think about the obstacles you have faced in your life. Think about the most trying times you have experienced. Didn't getting through those help to build who you are now? While you may not wish these things on someone, they probably helped you build strength and character. It's hard when you are in it. Let's face it, challenges suck. But if you approach an obstacle as something that will help you grow and learn, it will help you get to the other side.

If you need encouragement beyond your own life stories, learn more about other people. I love reading biographies of successful people. When you hear what they overcame, how they prevailed, it gives you inspiration for your own challenges.

While some obstacles, such as a death or natural disaster, come into our lives unavoidably, there is also a different kind of obstacle: one that we bring on ourselves. I'm talking about things such as overeating, not exercising, fighting with a spouse, constant over scheduling (yes, that is avoidable). Many of us will go our entire lives without ever overcoming those obstacles. But you can. With a plan. It's not enough to be aware of an obstacle. You need to give it its due focus and find a solution. I take on an obstacle like a challenge. There must be some way over, under, or around it.

Chances are you have wanted some version of that goal before. For example, maybe you wanted a few hours of quiet to yourself (and your Can-Do is a silent retreat). Or maybe you wanted to get paid for some advice you seem to give over and over (and your Can-Do is to start a business). What obstacles got in your way? They will get in your way again. So, let's take some time to think about an obstacle that you would need to overcome in order to accomplish your Can-Do item.

Overcoming Obstacles Exercise

This exercise will help you plan how to overcome an obstacle. Say, for example, that not having enough time in the day gets in the way of your exercise goals. You can put the following remedies in place and say "so long" to your problem.

If I don't have enough time, then I will book exercise on my calendar.
If I don't have enough time, I will do a twenty-minute workout at home.
If I don't have enough time, I will take a walk during my phone meeting.

List three obstacles that continue to get in the way of your Can-Do activity.

1. _____

2. _____

3. _____

Develop a plan for each one, and write it below:

1. *If* _____ *happens, then I will* _____

2. *If* _____ *happens, then I will* _____

3. *If* _____ *happens, then I will* _____

> When you come out of the storm you
> won't be the same person who walked in.
> That's what this storm's all about.
>
> **—HARUKI MURAKAMI**

Your plan will help you always walk out of the storm, turning your can't do into a can do, time and time again.

Failure

Were you tempted just now to skip this section? I'm proud of you for staying here. I promise I'll be gentle as we talk about failure, one big obstacle that most of us face more often than we want to admit. Most often the reason we don't go after something is because we are afraid we will fail. It gets quite personal. We don't want to look bad, and we sure don't want to feel like a failure.

Well, I want you to embrace failure. It is an opportunity to grow, get stronger, and learn. It might be terrifying at first—it'll get less scary as you practice failing. And when you fail, at least you will know you were trying. And, when you keep trying, chances are that eventually you will become successful at the very thing you originally failed at.

Right now, for example, I want to build my business as a speaker. I absolutely love getting a chance to speak to an audience. My podcast is great, but I don't get to see the audience, and sometimes it feels like I'm just talking to myself. I want a visible, live audience, because that's where I do my best work.

The problem is that I don't know much about the speaking business. I don't know if I need to get an agent or how to get engagements. But I have taken on a new personal challenge to take a chance to fail once a day. At some point every day, I am going to reach out and try to get a speaking engagement. I might get a no every day, but you know what? I bet, I just bet, that I will eventually get a yes.

Yes, I realize I receive many accolades for my successes. Yes, I have started a nationally recognized company, and I have written a book (well, two now), and I have created fitness DVDs. But do you know how many times I have failed? Of course you don't, because I don't flaunt every failure. None of us do! I get rejection on a daily basis, and it really is okay because I have reframed my definition of failure.

Let's look at the definition of failure.
Failure: *An event that does not accomplish its intended purpose; a person with a record of failing; someone who loses consistently. (Source: Vocabulary.com)*

By that definition, I'm a failure nearly every day! How often do you forget where you put your keys? Forget why you came downstairs? Misspell a word? We all fail, so we need to reframe the concept as something less negative.

Failure: *An opportunity to learn from an unwanted outcome so that you may be better in the future. (Source: Lisa Druxman Dictionary)*

That definition sounds much better, doesn't it? I felt like a failure a lot as a kid. It did not feel good, and I definitely did not embrace it. As I mentioned before, I didn't do well in school... or with friends... or in sports. Ugh. I still get a pit in my stomach when I think back to those times. But now, I see failure as something very different.

Motivational leader Tony Robbins says that failure is just a concept, and that our lives are controlled by the meaning we give things. You can look at a situation and say either, "that's the end of my career," or "that's just the beginning; a chance to try something different." If you think it's the end, you will respond and react very differently than if you think you are at the beginning. Remember: Failure is just a concept. You get to choose how to think about it and react to it.

How often have you given up because you failed or you were afraid to fail? Don't be afraid to fail; be afraid not to try. Failure is an opportunity to begin, only this time with more wisdom.

"If you've never failed, you've never tried anything new," Albert Einstein said. *But he's a genius!* you might be thinking. Einstein probably didn't feel like a genius when he failed at an early age. He didn't start to speak until he was nearly four years old. He didn't speak fluently until twelve. He was told by all of his teachers that he wouldn't amount to much. I think it's safe to say they were wrong.

Einstein wasn't the only successful person who failed plenty of times before his success. If you study the failures of famous people, you'll see there are very few overnight successes and even fewer successes that didn't fail at some time.

FAILURES OF SUCCESSFUL PEOPLE

1. **Abraham Lincoln** failed in politics and in business before becoming President.

2. **Dr. Seuss** received nearly thirty rejections before getting his first book published.

3. **The Beatles** were told that they had no future in music, and they were turned down by a very famous record company.

4. **Steven Spielberg** was a daydreamer (like me) and suffered from dyslexia. He was turned down by two major film schools due to his poor grades.

5. **Beethoven** had a music teacher who once told him that he was a hopeless composer.

6. **Babe Ruth** has the record for the most strikeouts (1,330 times)!

7. **Henry Ford** failed at business twice before he started The Ford Motor Company.

8. **Walt Disney** was turned down 302 times before getting financing for Disneyland. He was fired from a newspaper for having no imagination and no new ideas.

9. **Oprah Winfrey** was demoted from her job as a news anchor because the network thought she wasn't fit for television.

10. **J.K. Rowling** was turned town twelve times before a publisher took on Harry Potter.

I am motivated by the failures of other successful people because their examples help me realize that I can get through my own failures. I remember reading the story of Mary Kay (founder of Mary Kay Cosmetics) shortly after I started Stroller Strides. She was told that her idea would never work and that she would go bankrupt. She did fail at the beginning, but she stuck to her guns and revolutionized the cosmetics industry. If she could do it, so could I! So can you!

LET YOUR KIDS FAIL

It is also important to teach your kids about how people can overcome failure. I used to read my kids a wonderful book called *Salt in His Shoes: Michael Jordan and the Pursuit of A Dream*, by Deloris Jordan and Roslyn M. Jordan. It is the story of Michael Jordan and how he had failed terribly in basketball. Yes, failed in basketball. The most famous name in basketball was cut from his high school basketball team, but that failure motivated him to become the incredible success he turned out to be.

We live in a society now where everyone wins, and where kids are incredibly protected—both physically and emotionally. They aren't allowed to play in the street, and they have to wear elbow pads, knee pads, shin pads, and every other type of protective pads. True, there is wisdom in some of this protection, but we have to be careful not to overprotect. We have to let our children lose. We have to let them get hurt.

In her book *The Blessings of a Skinned Knee*, Wendy Mogel points out that we are overindulging our children. We give them too many things and too little structure, overnurturing them the whole way. Mogel suggests that we are trying to protect our kids from the pains of life and, in doing that, we may be keeping them from succeeding. We learn when we fail. The adults who had to overcome some level of adversity while growing up are the ones who have the greatest outcomes later in life. They learned from a young age how to engage their social support networks and develop the coping mechanisms necessary to negotiate life's challenges.

Let your kids lose at Monopoly.

Let them lose in sports.

Let them fall down and then show them how to get back up again.

EVEN FAILURE HAS ITS LIMITS

It's time to shift our perspective about failure from something to be avoided at all costs to something that facilitates our growth. When you are in the midst of failing, remind yourself that there is a lesson to be learned. I know it sucks when you are in it, but keep looking for the lesson. I should point out, though, that failing over and over is no badge of honor. Failing at a diet or exercise program time and time again isn't what I want you to embrace. The key question is whether you are learning from your failures and making changes. Some people call this *failing forward*.

HOW TO RECOVER FROM FAILURE

1. Review what happened.

2. Create a new plan.

3. Prepare to make a new mistake, but not the same one.

Einstein had to work hard for a long time to prove to his teachers that they were wrong. His genius was most certainly built on the foundation of his failures. Why? Because he learned from all of them.

A failure is not always a mistake, it may simply be the best one can do under the circumstances. The real mistake is to stop trying.

—B.F. SKINNER

Fail. Then fail again with something else. Don't stop trying.

Willpower

Training your brain to form new habits, shift your focus, and overcome obstacles takes something we've all heard plenty about: willpower. I find my clients often beat themselves up for not having enough of it. But, before you criticize yourself, consider that you might have plenty of willpower but you don't know how to maximize it.

Willpower is not a never-ending supply of oomph. I love how the book *The One Thing* describes willpower as a tank of gas. If you keep using it up, you will run out. The faster you go, the faster you use up the tank. Every time you make a decision, you use up your fuel. This is why you usually lose your willpower by the end of the day.

Stress and willpower don't mix. That's probably why you feel it's so low. People are so stressed out! If you want more willpower, you need to find ways to decrease your stress! Stress puts your brain in the fight-or-flight response. It cannot make wise, willpower kinds of decisions when it's in this mode.

Your brain uses glucose, just like your muscles do. And when you use your willpower, you use up a lot of that glucose. This might sound counterintuitive, but you need to feed your brain in order to keep your willpower up. When your sugar level is down in your brain, you can't focus and hence can't keep up your willpower. Eat healthy, balanced meals regularly and your brain will keep replenishing. Anything that boosts your mood, reduces stress, or increases your energy will also increase your willpower. So, once again, I'm encouraging you to do things that are good for you.

How else can you improve your willpower? Change your attitude. The mind will go where there is pleasure. So, if you attach a negative stigma to exercise or dieting, then you will resist. If you truly create positive associations with the activity and the result, then your mind will be attracted to that outcome. I'm not making this stuff up. Over the last five years, there has been incredible research on the science of willpower. Kelly McGonigal is a leading researcher in the field. She has a course at Stanford University called The Science of Willpower. Her analogy is the willpower is like a muscle. Just like a muscle, it can get fatigued if you use it continuously. But, just like a muscle, it can gain strength when you build it up slowly.

When you use willpower, your mind is in a battle between what you want now (to eat a treat or do anything instead of working out) and what you want in the future (to have a healthier physique). If you don't want the future goal badly enough, your willpower will always lose out. So, it's very important that you choose your goals wisely. Is it really important to you? Really? Do you have a very strong attachment to the outcome?

In my promise to be vulnerable with you, I will share a personal willpower challenge. I got in the habit of drinking a glass (or two) of wine each night. All day long, I would eat healthy, live healthy, and be super productive. And then sunset came and the craving for the glass of wine came. It had become a habit and, as we discussed earlier, habits are hard to break.

Still, I was surprised by my lack of willpower. I realized that my willpower muscles were totally fatigued by the end of the day. I live in such a state of productivity and work that my mind was exhausted by day's end. I have pretty much broken this habit now. I needed to change my attitude and feel a little more rested. I found that if I had a cup of tea and sat down for a minute before the evening of cooking and cleaning and homework that I was better prepared for a nonalcoholic evening! Now, instead of pouring a glass of wine, I pour a glass of kombucha into a wine glass.

Years ago I read a great book called *The Marshmallow Test: Mastering Self-Control* by Walter Mischel. In the early 1960s, Mischel ran an experiment with kids at Stanford University's nursery school. The children were told that they could have one marshmallow now, or they could wait and get more than one marshmallow later. The children were left alone with the one marshmallow in front of them. Pure torture, right? The kids who were able to wait distracted themselves with a variety of creative activities, while the kids who gave in were stressed and totally focused on the one marshmallow. Mischel studied these kids for fifty years and discovered something fascinating. The kids who had delayed their gratification had more willpower for the rest of their years, and they had lower weights, lower divorce rates, and higher SAT scores. If you glazed over this section, thinking "maybe I don't have the willpower gene so why bother paying attention," listen now: Mischel discovered that willpower is teachable!

As moms, in order to teach our kids willpower or delayed gratification, we have to model it. We can't expect our children to delay gratification if we don't. Let them see you hold off on buying the purse that you really want. Let them see you turn down the handouts at Costco. A bonus is that if you choose behaviors that have positive consequences, you are more likely repeat those behaviors.

**FIVE SCIENTIFICALLY PROVEN WAYS
TO INCREASE YOUR WILLPOWER**

1. **Find an accountability partner.** You are more likely to succeed if you have a spouse, friend, or team with the same goal as you. McGonigal has found that willpower is contagious. Be around other people who are successful.

2. **Have a healthy, enjoyable snack.** If you keep the blood sugar stable in your brain, the feeling of satisfaction will boost your willpower.

3. **Sleep.** Willpower is highest after sleep. So make sure to sleep well and even take a nap to refresh your willpower.

4. **Meditate or journal.** Do something to help you relax. It will give your brain the boost it needs.

5. **Have a success.** If you do something in baby steps and have success, your brain is more likely to keep on course.

We get so mad at ourselves for our lack of willpower. But it's not your will, it's your brain. This is all science! You can get your brain to lead you if you train it properly. Choose what's most important to you. Eat well. Stress less. Take small baby steps toward your goal. Get back on track when you get off track. This is doable!

Beating yourself up does you absolutely no good, and it only causes more stress in your brain. Stop! If you have a negative thought about yourself, stop and choose to move in the direction you actually want to go. Where there is a will, there is a way. You have both. And when your children see you having both, they will find their own will and their own way, too.

ADVERTISE TO YOURSELF

If you think willpower and training your brain is all about gritting your teeth and muscling through, I have a challenge for you. Collaborate with your brain more gently by advertising to yourself. Yes, you heard me right.

Advertisers spend billions of dollars to get their messages in front of you. They put messages on phones, computers, televisions, billboards, and on your texts. Why do they do this? Because it works. They can get people to believe that driving a certain car will make them cool and drinking a certain cocktail will make them sexy. So, why don't you consider advertising to yourself? YOU have control over where your eyes go far more than they do!

How often do you look at the back of your bathroom door? Your medicine cabinet? Your dashboard in your car? Or your computer screen? I am suggesting that you decide what you want to tell your brain. Print your favorite quotes, pictures, or poems, and hang them where you will see them over and over again. Remember that pathway in your brain? You get to choose the thoughts that will create the paths your brain most often travels. Advertise to yourself, and help create positive paths!

What's on the back of my bathroom door? Optimists International's Optimist Creed! I'll share it with you!

The Optimist Creed

Promise yourself

To be so strong that nothing can disturb your peace of mind.

To talk health, happiness, and prosperity to every person you meet.

To make all your friends feel that there is something in them.

To look at the sunny side of everything and make your optimism come true.

To think only of the best, to work only for the best, and to expect only the best.

To be just as enthusiastic about the success of others as you are about your own.

To forget the mistakes of the past and press on to the greater achievements of the future.

To wear a cheerful countenance at all times and give every living creature you meet a smile.

To give so much time to the improvement of yourself that you have no time to criticize others.

To be too large for worry, too noble for anger, too strong for fear, and too happy to permit the presence of trouble.

Monthly Challenge

May:

**Do a "do-over" redirection thought whenever
your inner gremlin speaks to you.
Do it over as a positive, can-do thought.**

Stop striving for perfection. Strive to be better than you were yesterday.
Don't just go through this year. Grow through it!

Chapter 6

Lead Like a Mom

This chapter is the result of my a-ha moments about moms and leadership. For the past two decades, I have immersed myself in the study of leadership and the study of motherhood. Just recently I began to realize how inter-twined the two are. I study leadership in order to develop my company, but I realize that what I've learned has been integral to how I am raising my family.

In this chapter, I will share with you some wisdom from some of my favorite leaders to show you how pow-erful and insightful leadership can be in motherhood. Leadership as a mom might mean that we give up some control—but do we really ever have control anyway? Or it might mean that we hold ourselves to higher standards as examples. Or that we let our children take the lead at times! Think about this for a minute. Scary, isn't it? But maybe also a little bit exciting, I hope.

What Is Leadership?

The Oxford Dictionary defines **leadership** as "the action of leading a group or an organization." In the broadest sense of the word, a leader is someone who brings people together and guides them toward a common goal. Anyone can tell others what to do, but effective leadership requires much more than the ability to assign tasks. There is plenty of debate about what the best kind of leadership looks like, but most agree that a true leader inspires his or her followers.

But wait, isn't that how we want to parent? Yes, my point exactly. Our most effective and brilliant moments as moms are those when we can step back from handing out tasks that dictate our children's activities and attention, and when we can step forward in a way that inspires our children, helps them learn, helps them grow from the inside out as well as the outside in.

Lead Like a Mom

Why do I study leadership so much? Is it because I'm a leader in my company? Why yes, but it's also because I've realized that these leadership lessons also apply to my role as a mom. While it sometimes feels like our role is no more than caring for the house, cooking, cleaning, and maybe going to work, we are in fact leaders in our family.

What would happen if you weren't around?
Who would your children become without your influence?
What would get done without your direction?

See, you are a leader. In fact, I think you will enjoy your role more as mom when you realize the effect you have on your family.

Now there is a very big difference between leading your family and leading a company. As the CEO of a company, one of the most important jobs I have is hiring the right people. As moms, we don't get to choose our kids. They are who they are, and we can't just replace them with a new hire. But we *can* raise them to be the best that they can be. Start with your family values and stay true to your family mission. (I'll explain more about this in chapter 10).

> *A leader is one who knows the way, goes the way, and shows the way.*
>
> —JOHN MAXWELL

It's up to us mamas. It's up to us to know the way, go the way, and show the way. It's up to us to lead our families.

What strengths do you have that help you as a leader in your family?

_____

_____

_____

I don't expect that you will dive in to the podcasts, books, and interviews that I have about leadership. So, I would like to share with you some of my favorite leadership lessons and help you see the connection to your own life.

ARIANNA HUFFINGTON

Let's start with Arianna Huffington. She is the co-founder and former editor-in-chief of *The Huffington Post* and the author of multiple books, including one of my favorites, *Thrive: The Third Metric to Redefining Success and Creating a Life of Well-Being, Wisdom, and Wonder*. Arianna said that the old definition of success was simply money and power.

"But it is like a two-legged stool, at some point you'll fall off of it." And Huffington literally did. She collapsed, and she was forced to look hard at her life and her health. She realized that a third metric needed to be added. She defines the third metric as well-being, wisdom, and wonder.

Are you about to fall off a proverbial stool? What are your two legs? Pinterest-worthy house and perfect kids? Maybe you need to redefine success for yourself and for your family. Perhaps you are too tied to metrics such as a tidy home, a certain weight on the scale, or an unrealistic expectation for perfect balance.

How about your vision of success for your kids? Do your metrics for your children's success only include things like a clean room, good grades, and being a star in sports? What about other metrics such as creativity, happiness, and health? Maybe it's time for us to focus more on them. It's up to us as the leaders of our families to cultivate new definitions of success.

What are your current definitions of success in your life?

1. _____
2. _____
3. _____

Are those realistic? Are they serving you? What new definitions might you consider?

1. _____
2. _____
3. _____

OPRAH WINFREY ON ADVERSITY

I can't talk about leadership without talking about Oprah Winfrey. The leadership lesson that Oprah has given me is about overcoming adversity. Oprah came from poverty. She was both physically and sexually abused. She gave birth to a stillborn baby at fourteen years old. She was told that she would never have a career in television. And yet, Oprah has become one of the most successful people of our time. Oprah triumphed over adversity.

What are we teaching our kids about turning around adversity? As moms—as leaders—we need to share stories about the people who have turned their struggles into opportunities. It is human nature to want easy. We all want the easy button. But easy does not often get us where we want to go. I bet some of the most valuable things and experiences of your life came from struggle. We are doing our children no favors by paving a perfectly easy road for them. I'm not saying that we should create struggle. Hard things happen all on their own. But we don't need to shelter our kids from the storm. Teach them to step into it.

What are some things that have been hard in your life? What did you learn from them? Have you shared those stories with your children?

SHERYL SANDBERG ON LEANING IN

Sheryl Sandberg is another leader you probably know. She is the COO of Facebook and the author of *Lean In: Women, Work, and the Will to Lead.* Sheryl was ranked number sixteen on *Fortune*'s "50 Most Powerful Women in Business" list. Even with all of that, I'm hesitant about listing her here as I'm not a total fan of the book. I feel like she is encouraging women to act more like men in order to move ahead. But I still think there is a take-away for moms. The old "wait till your father gets home" attitude does not position you as an effective leader in your family.

As moms, we need to lean in as a model for our kids. For instance, they should see us ask for what we want in work, in our relationships, and in life. Our kids need to observe us voicing what we need and expect for ourselves. At dinner, talk about how you asked for the raise or applied for a new position. Show your kids how to ask for help at home. We need to teach our kids to lean in, to use their voices and their strengths, and to go after their goals.

LEAD LIKE A MOM

127

It's tempting to do everything for our kids, but that truly does them no favors. Our role as parents is to teach our kids how to be self-sufficient, not overly dependent. I have a friend whose daughter didn't want to order her dinner at a restaurant and asked her mom to do so. My friend kindly but firmly told her daughter that she wouldn't be eating if she didn't speak up for herself. Tough? Maybe. But I'm guessing her daughter will grow up to be a woman who speaks up for herself confidently and clearly.

Encourage your kids to use their voices (respectfully, of course). Teach them to ask for what they want—and to be okay with it when you say no. Say yes when you can, so that your kids see the benefits of asking for what they need.

Where do you want to lean in in your life?

_____

_____

_____

_____

Where do you want your kids to lean in?

_____

_____

_____

_____

BRENÉ BROWN ON VULNERABILITY

Brené Brown is a professor specializing in studying vulnerability, courage, worthiness, and shame. Her books *Rising Strong*, *Daring Greatly* and *The Gifts of Imperfection* are all number one *New York Times* best sellers. And her TED Talk on vulnerability is a must watch—or listen to! (See page 221.)

Brown believes that "leadership has nothing to do with position, salary, or number of direct reports." She believes, instead, that "a leader is anyone who holds her- or himself accountable for finding potential in people and processes." Finding the potential in people. I wish that could be the new definition for motherhood. Isn't that what we do? See the potential in our children?

> *Vulnerability is indeed at the core of difficult emotions, but it is also the birthplace of love and belonging, joy, creativity and innovation, adaptability to change and accountability–the experiences that bring purpose and meaning to our lives.*
>
> —BRENÉ BROWN

I think vulnerability may be a big part of what is missing from motherhood. We put a mask on and act like everything is peachy keen. We are stoic for our children. And while I think it's important that we are strong leaders, I am not sure that it behooves us to protect our vulnerability. Vulnerability is very difficult for people, and yet is at the core of how we connect to one another. Vulnerability is not taught anywhere. It's truly up to us as moms to model what it looks like.

Your family will respond when you share your needs and ask for help before you explode. Being vulnerable, by the way, is in no way being weak! It takes incredible courage and strength to allow our true selves to show up every day. I have shown my vulnerability with my family by sharing stories of how I had trouble making friends a kid. I share my vulnerability by letting my family know that sometimes I don't think I'm doing the best job as a mom or as a wife. I don't say it to complain. I share to connect and to be real.

By the way, Brown says that she doesn't believe in parenting experts as there are a million ways to be a great parent. Her message is to be who you want your kids to be. Hmmm, sounds familiar, doesn't it? That really ups the ante on our responsibility as leaders of our family.

How do you show vulnerability to your family?

_____

_____

_____

_____

Has it been helpful? Where might you be more vulnerable?

_____

_____

_____

_____

TONY ROBBINS ON BRINGING OUT PEOPLE'S GREATNESS

Last, but certainly not least, I want to talk about motivational writer and speaker Tony Robbins. As many of you who have followed my blog and podcast know, Tony Robbins was my first. Well, the first person I started following to learn about self-development and leadership, that is! Tony believes that the ultimate definition of a true leader is simply "someone who inspires others to become more of who they truly are."

Robbins tells us that a true leader brings out the greatness that's in each human being and helps them to consistently put that greatness into practice. "Leaders influence themselves and others to do, be, give, and become more than they ever thought possible," he says. That's the gift that we can give ourselves and bestow on our kids. We should not be raising them as mirror images of who we are. We should lead them to be the greatness that is within them by giving them examples of how we find the greatness within us.

We all have greatness. Maybe you see it as your gift or your strength. Maybe you are amazing at cooking or at planning fundraisers. My gift is being a dreamer, an idea person. My kids see that I turn my dreams into reality as I share my ideas for podcasts, books, and new programs. I share my failures, and hopefully they see how I get back up again. They see me turning down opportunities that would be good for the business but not good for our family. I can only hope that it is inspiring them to find the greatness within themselves.

Even as I write this, I'm aware of how hard it is to acknowledge the greatness within. Who am I to be great? Well actually, as Marianne Williamson said, who am I not?

> *"Our deepest fear is not that we are inadequate. Our deepest fear is that we are powerful beyond measure. It is our light, not our darkness that most frightens us. We ask ourselves, 'Who am I to be brilliant, gorgeous, talented, fabulous?' Actually, who are you not to be? You are a child of God. Your playing small does not serve the world. There is nothing enlightened about shrinking so that other people won't feel insecure around you. We are all meant to shine, as children do. We were born to make manifest the glory of God that is within us. It's not just in some of us; it's in everyone. And as we let our own light shine, we unconsciously give other people permission to do the same."*
> —**Marianne Williamson, *A Return to Love: Reflections on the Principles of "A Course in Miracles"***

Where is there greatness within you?

_____

_____

_____

_____

_____

Some may say that people are either born a great leader or not, but I disagree. I believe that leadership can be taught, and, with practice, we can each become a highly effective leader. I hope you will take that to heart as you see the potential for leadership greatness within you.

A leader is best when people barely know she* exists.
When her* work is done, her* aim fulfilled,
they will say: we did it ourselves.

—LAO TZU

*Originally masculine pronouns

How Moms Can Be Great Leaders

Such an important topic needs a handy list, so here are some of the significant ways that moms lead their families:

1. Define what success looks like in your family. In my family, it's about best effort; it's not about being the best. What is success for you? Does your family know this definition?

2. Don't protect your children from failure. Teach them how to get back up again when they fall.

3. Don't be afraid to lead. Saying "wait till your father gets home" takes away from your own strength in the family.

4. Teach your kids to lean in, to use their voices, to ask for what they want.

5. Involve your kids in goal setting and family planning. Let them see that results come from work and from planning for success.

6. Don't be afraid to be vulnerable with your kids. Show them that sometimes you are uncertain or don't have the answer.

7. Help your children find the greatness that lies within them.

June:

Create a list of ways you show leadership as a mom. Choose one additional leadership attribute to practice this month.

Stop striving for perfection. Strive to be better than you were yesterday.

Don't just go through this year. Grow through it!

Chapter 7

Fuel for You and Your Family

So far, we've looked closely at your thoughts and at your role as a leader in your family. Now we turn to something that is equally important and easily ignored: Your brain is part of your physical body. What you eat affects your brain and your whole body. We are a fast-food nation where obesity and diabetes are epidemics. It's time to slow down and pay attention to how we use food and mealtimes in our families.

I believe that good food can be the foundation of your happy and healthy life. For years, I thought I ate pretty healthy. That was until I started eating really healthy. Then I realized how much food fuels my happy and healthy life. In this chapter, I'll provide information and exercises to do with your family to help them understand and appreciate their food.

Why Healthy Eating Matters

I've talked a lot so far about the role your thoughts and decisions play in your overall health and leadership in your family. What we don't often think much about is our brains. Your brain is a physical part of your body, and what you eat is important for your physical health and for your mental health as well.

You would think that because I'm a fitness professional that I would choose to write about fitness before food, but that's not the case. Did you know that 80 percent of your health comes from your food? Okay, truth be told I can't find a source for this, but I bet it's true!

If you are what you eat, what are you? What are your kids? Is your daughter made up of goldfish crackers and chicken nuggets? Is your son made up of burgers and fries? Are you made up of packaged diet shakes and fast food? Hopefully not, but don't feel bad if you are. We live in a packaged, fast-food, processed world. Most of what we eat isn't really food. I have challenged my clients to go an entire day without eating a processed food, and many were shocked at how difficult it was.

Do you feel truly healthy? Alive? Thriving? Or are you merely not sick? *Not sick is not the same as healthy.* You can set yourself up for health and positive energy by eating a balanced, whole-food diet.

What do I mean by processed foods? If you slice up apples and bake them, are they processed? Nope. Processed foods are foods have been chemically processed and are made up of artificial and refined ingredients. So, a baked apple is a whole food; a prepackaged apple fruit leather with loads of preservatives is not.

Why are whole foods so important? When you eat a whole food, your body knows exactly how to digest it. It knows how to absorb the nutrients, use the fiber, then pass on what it doesn't need. When you eat processed food, your body has no idea how to deal with the chemical shit storm. (Sorry for the cursing; it's the only time I'll do it.) My friend Leah Segedie, founder of Mamavation, calls it CSS for short. Processed food is not only making people fat, it's causing an abundance of disease.

Let's take a real-life example. Let's say I see a banana on my counter. I'm hungry, so I decide to eat it. It's a perfect food that comes in its own wrapper. I enjoy it. I feel satisfied. Will I reach for another? Probably not; never in my life have I binged on bananas. Now, let's look at another scenario. I decide to eat a bag of chips. They are very enjoyable. I want more, so I empty the bag or go for another food. Our natural instincts are disturbed when we eat processed foods. We don't know when we are full, and in many instances the foods are created to make us crave more. Look in your pantry right now. I bet that 70 percent of your foods are processed. The closer a food that you eat is to its whole state, the closer you will be to a healthy body.

Need more reasons to avoid processed foods? Keep reading, and see page 221 for recommended movies on healthy eating.

BE AWARE

I'll touch on a few of the dangers of eating processed foods here. I hope you will read through these and consider removing them from your family's diet—or at least reducing them.

Artificial Colors and Preservatives: Many artificial colors and preservatives have been tied to autism, ADHD, eczema, mood swings, headaches, obesity, diabetes, cancer, and hyperactivity.

Trans Fats: These are also known as trans-fatty acids, and they can be found in hydrogenated oil. These result from adding a hydrogen atom to vegetable oil for a longer shelf life. You can find trans fats in baked goods, fried foods, refrigerated dough, creamers, and margarine. We know that it raises your LDL (bad cholesterol) and lowers your HDL (good cholesterol).

Sugar: Sugar is potentially the worst ingredient in the modern diet. It is high in calories, yet offers absolutely ZERO nutritional benefit and can have harmful effects on your metabolism and contribute to multiple diseases. When sugar enters your bloodstream, it is broken down into fructose and glucose. Fructose can only be metabolized by the liver, and if you eat too much sugar it can overload your liver, forcing it to turn the fructose into fat. Keep doing this and it can lead to fatty liver disease. Sugar can also cause insulin resistance—the first step before diabetes or metabolic syndrome. There is considerable evidence that sugar can lead to cancer.

Knowing all this, why do we eat sugar? Because it is addictive. Sugar causes a dopamine response, much like recreational drugs. How much sugar should you have? The American Heart Association recommends a maximum of 25 grams of added sugar (6 teaspoons) per day. Compare that to the 76 grams of sugar per day that the average person in America eats. That's 19 teaspoons of sugar!

High-Fructose Corn Syrup (HFCS): The average American ingests 60 pounds of HFCS per year. Is it a coincidence that we have the highest rates of obesity and diabetes ever? The Corn Refiners Association will try to convince you that HFCS is the same as natural sugar, but biochemically it is not. Glucose and fructose are separated, sending fructose directly to your liver. It contains mercury, and it may lead to fatty liver and various intestinal issues. Why do they use it? To make products sweeter and cheaper to produce. It's in virtually every processed food and sugary drink. It is a red flag for everything bad for you. Toss out all foods with HFCS.

Be careful. All of the following ingredients you see on food labels are sugar. Don't let the name fool you.

- Cane sugar
- Corn syrup
- Crystalline fructose
- Dextrose
- Evaporated cane juice
- Fructose
- Glucose
- High-fructose corn syrup
- Agave nectar
- Malt syrup
- Molasses
- Raw sugar
- Sucrose

Genetically modified organisms (GMOs): GMOs have been around for thousands of years. We got the sweet potato because a farmer figured out how to modify the root of a potato. Farmers have long been "breeding" the best of their crops to create stronger crops. I'm not concerned about those techniques.

The GMOs that I'm concerned with are the ones that have genes introduced into them in a laboratory from an organism of a totally unrelated species. These GMOs are supposed to reduce the use of pesticides, reduce greenhouse emissions, increase food production for developing countries, and enable the organisms to manipulate nutrients. Sounds good, right? Wrong. There is evidence that this tampering with nature is causing havoc on our bodies. Do you want to eat corn that is also considered a pesticide?

There is zero research showing that GMO foods are safe for us. We do know that thousands of sheep died from eating a GMO crop. Doesn't that tell you something? Numerous countries have banned GMOs or at least demanded labeling, but not the United States. We are part of a grand experiment, and we have no idea if GMOs are part of our food. The research has shown:

- Multiple toxins from GMOs have been found in fetal blood.
- Gluten disorder is most likely connected to GMOs.
- Studies have shown an increase in tumors in rats who eat GMOs.
- Alzheimer's, Parkinson's, and autism are linked to GMOs.

I know this can be hard to hear, especially if your diet is filled with these foods. You might also be thinking that I'm an extremist or an alarmist, but a lot of the research is indicating this is true. It is unfortunate that our food industry makes it so difficult to stay away from harmful ingredients, but don't make yourself crazy about it. Any certified organic product or product with a Non-GMO Project label can be considered safe. Just be aware and be educated, then take baby steps toward what you feel is reasonable. For more information on GMOs, check out the resources section on page 221.

GMO Awareness Exercise

List all of the foods that your child has eaten in the last day. Check off how many of them fall under these "food beware" categories.

	GMO FOOD	HIGH SUGAR	TRANS FATS
_____	❏	❏	❏
_____	❏	❏	❏
_____	❏	❏	❏
_____	❏	❏	❏
_____	❏	❏	❏
_____	❏	❏	❏
_____	❏	❏	❏
_____	❏	❏	❏
_____	❏	❏	❏
_____	❏	❏	❏
_____	❏	❏	❏
_____	❏	❏	❏
_____	❏	❏	❏

Learn the Facts

This section will help you continue your education about food in the United States. Plain and simple, we are killing our country and we are preying on our vulnerable children. Again, I am not an extremist; this is real and supported by scientific research. We are the first generation to be told that our children will have a shorter life expectancy than we have! America has the highest obesity rate in the world, and the countries that are runners-up are obese because they are eating an American-style diet. (See the resources on page 221 for more information.)

The documentary *Fed Up* produced by Katie Couric and Laurie David shared some staggering statistics about the quality (or lack of it) of our food.

+ Ninety percent of the food in our supermarkets is not food.
+ Kids watch ten food-related ads per day, and none of them are for fruits or vegetables.
+ The food companies that are hurting us are spending forty million dollars per year on lobbying the federal government.
+ Every store—gas stations, electronics stores, and even art supply stores—bombards us with processed foods at the checkout.
+ Congress has been lobbied by the food industry to prevent full disclosure of nutrition labels.
+ Manufacturers of corn-based sweeteners, such as high-fructose corn syrup, have benefited from billions of dollars of subsidies.
+ A 20-ounce (591 ml) bottle of soda has approximately 17 teaspoons (71 g) of sugar. That is about three times the total amount of sugar we should have in a day.
+ Schools cafeterias across America have turned into fast food and soda distributors.
+ Ninety-three million Americans are affected by obesity.
+ Kids are sent home with report cards that have pictures of Ronald McDonald on them, promising a free Happy Meal for good grades.
+ Sugar is added to more than 80 percent of processed foods.

By 2050, one in three Americans will have diabetes. This is not okay! It is our job as parents to leave a better legacy for our children. They should not be left with the legacy of shorter life expectancies than their parents.

Eating real food is not elitist, and it can be affordable. We all need to go back to eating real food. Start a ripple effect, please. Learn, share, and demand a change. You are worth it and your children deserve it.

MEAL TIME

Meal time is not just a "nice to have" in your family; it is essential to your family's health. This is a very fast-paced world, so it is more important than ever that we sit down as a family to eat. But families today rarely do that: The average American eats one in five meals in her car, and the majority of American families eat less than one meal per week together.

Moms often ask me to look at their daughter's diets, concerned because their daughters don't eat enough, eat too much, or eat poorly. When I ask for the mom's food diary, she'll often say, "It's not me, it's my daughter." But those food diaries often tell me that it is the mom—not the daughter—who has some food issues. Most of the time, the mom is dieting, doing a cleanse, or trying the latest fad diet ... and they are rarely sitting down to eat with their kids.

We must model healthy eating. We must show our kids that food is fuel. We must show that we enjoy food and savor it. Food can be powerful, but should not have power over us.

Studies show that children who do not eat with their parents:

+ are more likely to be obese.
+ perform less well in school.
+ have more truancies.
+ have more trouble with drugs and alcohol.

I'm not saying that this is a cause and effect, and perhaps it's just a correlation. But I do know that eating together gives families a chance to connect. The biggest excuse for not eating healthy meals is time, but in chapter 3 you learned several ways to manage your time. Now, make healthy eating a priority.

1. Set aside one day each week to do your meal planning.

2. Go food shopping and set yourself up for success.

3. Set aside an hour or two on the weekend to pre-prep some meals. For example, precut veggies and grill some chicken.

4. Pick one night of the month to have a moms' night out where you all make and take meals for the month. Each person makes multiple servings of one dish, and then you trade.

5. As a last resort, if you're caught off guard for that night's dinner, buy precut veggies and roasted chicken so you don't have to cook. What matters is that you are eating real food and that you are eating together!

Check out the resources on page 221 for more information on this topic.

Never Too Early

Many people would be surprised to find out how early our nutritional habits begin. New research shows that a baby's "taste" for certain foods can begin in the womb. That may explain Jacob's affinity for sushi! For this reason, you want to eat a variety of healthy foods during your pregnancy and avoid sugars, salts, and processed foods.

Those same tastes develop as your baby enjoys your breast milk. Research also suggests that breastfed babies may be less picky eaters as kids (and into adulthood) than formula-fed infants, especially if mom eats a balanced diet while nursing.

Many new moms are not sure what foods to feed baby when they start eating solid foods, so they turn to processed baby foods and children's menus. A study of more than 3,000 kids under age two found that many babies and toddlers have already developed an appetite for hot dogs, french fries, candy, and soda. This is very disconcerting considering that a child's food preferences are set in the first three years of life!

It's pretty easy to make your own baby food. If that's too overwhelming, though, there are great organic baby food brands such as Earth's Best, Happy Family, Plum Organics, and Ella's Kitchen.

CHILDREN'S MENUS BEWARE

Have you ever noticed the selection of foods on kids menus? Everything is fried and filled with saturated fats. Chicken nuggets, macaroni and cheese, burgers, and fries. Why do we wonder about obesity rates in children?

Kids should be eating whole, unprocessed foods—and so should you. Instead of ordering off the kiddie menu, order one regular main course and split it with your child, adding extra veggies or a healthy side-dish if you need more food.

TO JUICE OR NOT TO JUICE?

You may be wondering whether it is healthy to serve your kids fruit juice. It sounds healthy because it is fruit, after all, but be aware that fruit juices often contain a lot of sugar. Fruit juice causes an immediate blood sugar spike. If you do give your kids juice, serve only 100 percent fruit juice. One 4- to 6-ounce (120- to 180-ml) serving a day is plenty for babies, toddlers, and children age six and under. Kids age seven and over may drink up to 12 ounces (455 ml) a day. Also consider diluting fruit juice with water to cut calories. Better yet, if your child is thirsty, serve milk or water, and let them get their fruit juice from the actual fruit!

What If Your Family Isn't on Board?

So now you are motivated and excited to change your eating habits, but what if your family doesn't support your change? A mom recently told me that her husband didn't want to eat "bird food" and that her kids aren't happy with the healthy food she prepares. What can she do?

First of all, healthy eating isn't "bird food," it is real food. If you join my Body Back program, you will find a ton of delicious foods in our journal. The majority of recipes there are what I make for my own family. Make sure, however, not to put your family on a diet. Just get them—and you—eating healthier whole foods.

Try also to empathize with your family, because they didn't ask to change. Your husband might be questioning why you're changing, so don't force him to eat what you are eating or to change his ways if he is not ready. Do let him know that it's important to you, and tell him specifically how he can support YOU. Ask him not to tempt you with foods or pressure you to make unhealthy choices.

As for your kids, it is a gift for them to get them eating whole foods. Try to give them healthy choices. Don't force them to eat anything, but also don't let yourself become a short-order cook. In my opinion, you only need to make one dinner, not different foods for different family members. Of course, you may make adjustments for allergies or if something is too spicy. But, in general, there are plenty of options that everyone can learn to enjoy. Try to get your family excited about lots of new food choices. Keep your kitchen stocked with good foods and no one will feel deprived.

Better yet, why not make healthy eating FUN for your kids? I'll get you started.

TIPS FOR MAKING HEALTHY EATING FUN FOR KIDS

+ Egg Slicer: Toddlers love having their hard-boiled eggs in pretty, neat slices. But that's not all this slicer can do. Use it to slice strawberries, mushrooms, kiwi, and more.
+ Melon Baller: Kids like bite-size foods. Use your melon baller to slice melons, papaya, mangos, and more.
+ Cookie Cutter: Use a cookie cutter to make sandwich shapes more fun. Try using special cutters to make fun-size pieces of food (See page 221 for resources.)

- Spiralizer: A spiralizer can make "noodles" out of vegetables, such as zucchini and carrots.
- Focus on color. Make a rainbow with naturally bright, beautiful fruits and vegetables.
- Tie in to kids' interests. I used to make an Incredible Hulk green smoothie for Jacob.
- Serve food differently. Get bento boxes for kids who like to keep foods separate. Use toothpicks or skewers. For example, I used to make lollipop meatballs where I put lollipop sticks into the meatballs.
- Finally, and most importantly, involve your kids in the food prep!

Imagine that I gave you your dream car for free. What would it be? Porsche? BMW? Ferrari? Now there is just one catch. You get it for free, but this is the only car you can drive for the rest of your life. I bet you would take pretty good care of that car! You would keep it clean, put the best gas in it, and keep up on all the routine maintenance.

Isn't your body that same dream car? It's an amazing machine, and it's the only one you will get for your entire life. You need to take incredible care of it, and food is a big part of that care. The saying that you are what you eat is pretty much true. When you put good foods in, good energy and health comes out. And, as a leader of your family, it is up to you to feed your family well and be a role model with your own health.

July:

Do a kitchen clean up. Toss out foods with artificial sweeteners, high-fructose corn syrup, and various CSS (chemical @#%! storm) foods. Eat at least one fresh, whole food at every meal.

Stop striving for perfection. Strive to be better than you were yesterday.
Don't just go through this year. Grow through it!

Chapter 8

The Strength for Motherhood

We all know that we should exercise, yet exercise is often the first thing to go when time is tight. This chapter will motivate you to add exercise into your regular schedule in a way that you can manage long term. I will share exercise tips to make your workouts productive within the time you have, and I will show you how you can fit workouts in with your family no matter their ages.

The Facts

Technically, my company is a fitness company, so I am obviously biased about moms working out. Stroller Strides is a total body workout where moms work out as they push their kids in a stroller. A certified instructor leads the moms through a stroller walk (or run), and they stop along the way to do strength stations. For instance, they might do push-ups at a park table, lunges with the stroller, or bicep curls with an exercise tube.

Creating Stroller Strides was an interesting epiphany for me. As a fitness professional for more than twenty years, I was always told that more than 80 percent of America didn't work out. When I started Stroller Strides, I tapped into that 80 percent through many women who had never set foot in a gym but came to class. What got them there? One, they liked the idea of being outdoors with their babies. Two, many of them came more to connect than to work out. The fitness was icing on the cake. And three, the moms who were once avid gym-goers, but now no longer had time to get away to work out, had to find their new normal.

Two facts:
1. Moms need to work out. You need the strength, energy, and endorphins.
2. Your workout needs to change with the different stages of motherhood.

As you know, motherhood comes with a unique set of obstacles, especially as your body changes from pregnancy and giving birth, not to mention how active we need to be to keep up with our kids. One challenge is that fitness for motherhood is not a "one size fits all" solution. So let's talk more about different stages and different exercise options.

FITNESS AT ANY STAGE

All moms want their bodies back after baby, but most have trouble fitting it in. As a mother, you have very little leftover time available. Like none. So you need to figure out innovative ways to work out during each stage of motherhood. If you enjoy going to the gym and are able to squeeze that into your routine, then you are all set—all the power to you! If, on the other hand, you want to cry at the thought of adding "go to the gym" to your life, I have some simple alternatives for you. But first, let's start with motivation and some important things you should know before you dive back into your workouts.

WHY YOUR WORKOUT SHOULD CHANGE WITH MOTHERHOOD

All moms should get doctor's clearance to exercise after birth of baby. Most doctors will clear a mom at six weeks. It may be longer for moms with a contraindication or who had a cesarean.

Whether you like it or not, your life and your body will change after having a baby, so your workout needs to change too. Being a mom is simply hard on your body. As a mom, you have a weight (the baby) that you carry around everywhere you go. You're sleep deprived, recovering from pregnancy and labor, and doing all kinds of mommy movements that you have not done before. This combination can lead to new aches and pains and progressively poor posture. By learning how to move through motherhood and working out to address these new challenges, you will be stronger, healthier, and happier.

Postural changes: Many changes have happened to your body during pregnancy. The weight of your uterus, your baby, and your growing breasts have probably pulled your posture out of alignment. Your hips have probably tilted forward (an anterior pelvic tilt) and your shoulders have probably rounded. Your head gets pulled along and juts forward, too.

Almost 80 percent of women complain of back pain during or after pregnancy. Much of that pain comes from this postural misalignment. To counteract this and help realign your posture, your workout should focus on strengthening your core, glutes and back muscles and it should stretch your chest and hip flexors.

Your pelvic floor: Your pelvic floor muscles support your bladder and other pelvic organs. The weight of the baby and uterus, as well as the process of childbirth, have probably weakened your pelvic floor. As a result, you might have problems controlling your bladder. I'm pretty sure none of us likes leaking pee when we cough or laugh, right? That is why Kegel and other pelvic floor exercises are important not only during pregnancy but throughout your life after having a baby. Pelvic rehabilitation is a type of physical therapy for your pelvic floor, and it is often recommended if you have symptoms or pain. Don't be embarrassed! This is common and you want to restore those muscles so you don't have a lifetime of problems.

Your tummy: Are your abs ever going to look the same again? Not without targeted work, because you lost great strength in your abs during pregnancy. I was so devastated to see that I still looked pregnant after having Jacob. I had to wear my maternity clothes for at least another month! Your abdominal muscles had to stretch out quite a bit to cover that growing baby and uterus. You need to build your abs back up by working core exercises into most of your exercise routines. This is not just about sit-ups. In fact, the best core workouts don't happen on the ground. You can do woodchops, balance movements, and resisted rotation to strengthen your core. Of course, planks, side planks, and bird dog are great floor exercises. No idea what I'm talking about? Visit fit4mom. com/bookinsider for links to these exercises.

WHY DO I FEEL WORSE NOW
THAN WHEN I WAS PREGNANT?

There are many possible reasons for not feeling good after having a baby. As if postpartum depression, lack of sleep, and feeling overwhelmed are not enough, you also have many new movements of motherhood to cause you discomfort.

- **Pushing a stroller:** Most moms hunch over when pushing a stroller. It's important to use good posture and form, standing up comfortably straight (spine in neutral) with shoulders down and back. Think about leading with your chest and keeping your shoulders in your back pockets!

- **Carrying your baby:** Make sure to balance the amount of time you hold your baby on each side. Holding your baby on your hip with one arm can cause muscular imbalances, so switch up right side and left side frequently. I can still feel the pain deep in my shoulder girdle from always holding Jacob on my left side.

- **Nursing/Feeding:** Hunching over to feed your baby will give you back and posture problems. Bring your baby up to you using a pillow or nursing props and a proper chair. I remember getting into the most contorted positions just to get my baby to latch on. Take a breath. Get in a position that is comfortable for you. If you are having any trouble nursing, get a lactation consultant. Best money you will ever spend!

- **Carrying a car seat:** Unfortunately, these indispensable items also wreak havoc on our bodies. Hold your car seat carrier in front of you—like a laundry basket—whenever possible so that your body is balanced. If you hold it with one arm, be careful to keep your spine in neutral alignment. Just like holding baby, be sure to switch sides if you use one arm. And hey, work on your bicep strength while you are at it!

✦ **Wearing a front pack carrier:** Worn incorrectly, this carrier can be a postural pain. Worn correctly, however, it can be a great workout. Your front pack carrier should have a snug fit and supportive back straps. Your posture is most important when wearing a front pack carrier. Keep your spine in neutral and abs pulled in. Make sure to pull your shoulders back; don't leave them rounded forward.

Now that you are aware of these movements of motherhood, you can make slight adjustments and soon create habits more aligned with comfort and strength. (See what I did there?) You will soon have those basics mastered, so let's talk about other exercises. Choose your fitness program based on your stage of motherhood.

Newborn to Three Months

Your old workout most certainly does not fit into your new life, but that does not mean you're off the hook. It's time to build a foundation and bring your body back into alignment. Exercises such as Kegels and abdominal bracing are great to start restoring your core and pelvic floor. You should also start walking, slowly building up the intensity and length of each walk. My best new-mama moments were out on a stroller walk with my babies.

Three Months to One Year

There is not a lot of "mom time" in the first year of motherhood. You need to squeeze fitness into the nooks and crannies of the day. Mommy and baby workouts are a great way to get in some exercises. For example, you can chest press with baby or do reverse curls with baby on your legs. You can also get a great workout with baby in a front pack carrier. Squats and lunges are even more effective with the added baby weight!

Motherhood can sometimes feel lonely. Try a stroller workout class to get in shape and get some fresh air. When on your own stroller walk, you can up the intensity by adding more hills and strength intervals, such as squats and lunges, but don't be too hard on yourself or push yourself too fast. Your body went through many changes during pregnancy—give it time to build back up, focusing on your core and pelvic floor strength. And, of course, I would love to invite each and every one of you to Stroller Strides. Go to page 220 for a link for a free week of classes.

One to Three Years

Your stroller workouts may still be the best bet for time and enjoyment with baby. As your baby gets bigger, you'll get stronger! At this stage, you can also pop in a workout DVD or try out one of the many free workouts available online. Your toddler may have fun trying to join you! Hopefully, you are no longer sleep deprived and can sneak in a workout while your little one naps. Virtually all of motherhood pulls your body forward; pushing a stroller, nursing, holding baby. At this stage, focus on back strength and posture exercises.

Three to Five Years

Your little one is more mobile and you can be, too. Go for a run as you help push them along on a bike. Play red-light, green-light and tag at the park. The playground is a great place to work out. Do some step-ups, push-ups, and dips on the park bench. Don't be tempted to sit around while your kids are playing—join them instead. When your kids start school, you can go back to the gym or your favorite workout class.

Six+ Years

From here on, anything is possible, and you can include your family in your workout routine for some fun bonding. For instance, there are a number of sports that you can play with your kids. Try tennis, karate, or yoga. Create a circuit workout at the park for you and your family. If your child plays a team sport, you can use that time to go for a run around the field or do your own workout. You want your kids to grow up seeing that you exercise and that you love it. Include them as much as possible so that they can grow up to be healthy and fit!

No matter your stage of motherhood, fitness is a gift for you and your family. YOU need the strength in motherhood! And they need to learn from you that fitness is fun and an important part of daily life.

Types of Training

What do I do for my own workouts? Well I'm glad you asked! I love running and yoga, but what is essential for me is HIIT training and resistance training.

HIGH INTENSITY INTERVAL TRAINING

If you have heard of HIIT workouts before and wondered what in the world they are, here's your answer: HIIT stands for "high intensity interval training." The concept is to alternate short intervals of exercise at a very high intensity with intervals of rest. The intense interval could be anywhere from eight seconds to eight minutes, and it is not an exercise that you could do at a steady state for forty-five minutes, like an aerobics class or going for a jog. The rest period is low intensity exercise, such as walking or just slight movement, and it can also vary in time.

BENEFITS OF HIIT

Why in the world would you want to put yourself through this intensity? Well, for one thing, most moms are short on time, and you can get an effective HIIT workout in as little as twenty minutes. And of course there are plenty of health benefits.

HIIT training can improve your:

- aerobic and anaerobic fitness (lower intensity and higher intensity)
- blood pressure
- cardiovascular health
- insulin sensitivity
- cholesterol profiles (LDL, HDL, triglycerides, and total cholesterol)
- amount of abdominal fat and body weight while maintaining muscle mass

One of the most popular benefits of HIIT training is the EPOC (excess post-exercise oxygen consumption). The phrase is a mouthful, but the concept is simple. Think about your car, how the engine stays warm for a bit after you run it. In the same way, your body stays warm after exercise, and after a high intensity workout, your body takes even longer to cool down, burning calories the whole time as it replaces the oxygen used up during the workout. Put simply, exercise that consumes more oxygen burns more calories, so your HIIT workout can also help you lose weight and increase lean body mass.

CAUTION: HIIT workouts should only be done one to three times per week! More is not better! A true HIIT workout should exhaust you, so doing too many HIIT workouts increases your chance of injury. Also, "overdosing" on HIIT can cause stress on your body, which releases the stress hormone cortisol. Over time, having this cortisol hanging out in your body can cause a host of health problems and it can increase fat gain around the abdomen—that is certainly not what we were going for! But don't throw out the baby with the bath water, either. If you keep to a healthy number of HIIT workouts, the benefits far outweigh the potential issues.

HIIT workouts are efficient and effective when you do them one to three times per week. This is how we designed our Body Back program, so consider using that as a specific guide. Fill your other days with a combination of aerobic cardio (Stroller Strides, jogging, swimming), strength (Stroller Strides, weights, body weight exercise) and flexibility (Stroller Strides, yoga, stretching). Again, with HIIT workouts, more is not better. Better is better.

Go to page 220 for a link to my website for a free twenty-minute HIIT workout video. It will hurt so good!

RESISTANCE TRAINING

All moms (all people, for that matter) should do resistance training. Proper resistance training will improve your posture, your strength, and your ability to burn fat. The increase in lean body mass leads to more metabolically active tissue, meaning you are burning more calories each and every day!

You don't need a health club or special equipment to do these seven key resistance exercises.

SEVEN ESSENTIAL RESISTANCE EXERCISES

- Push-ups
- Squats
- Sit-ups
- Dips
- Lunges

- Planks/side planks
- Pull-ups (Yes, women can do pull-ups! Get a pull-up bar or pull-up strap for these.)

Go to page 220 for a link to that show you how to do each exercise correctly. Even if you are familiar with the exercises, I recommend watching the video as a refresher on correct form.

We've talked in earlier chapters about the concept of small steps forward. Remember, baby steps will get you anywhere you want to go. Consider a baby-step workout. Grab a piece of graph paper and put down the exercises you want to see an improvement on. Every time you do those exercises, see if you can add one more rep or one more second. You will love seeing the improvement, no matter how small. And those small steps will add up.

	January 5	January 14		
Push-Ups	2	3		
Squats	15	18		
Sit-Ups	12	13		
Dips	20	23		
Lunges	12	14		
Plank	30 seconds	28 seconds		
1 Mile Run	11 minutes	10 minutes		

Oops! Looks like our plank time went down. That's okay! We aren't perfect and our times won't always increase, but the important thing is that we keep trying.

Frequently Asked Questions About Exercise

I hear some of the same important questions time and time again from moms. Here are some of the top questions and answers about fitness.

What's the best time to work out?
Any time when you will actually do it! I am a huge proponent of early morning workouts if it fits your schedule. I find that it sets your energy for the day, and it eliminates the chance of you finding an excuse not to do it. (See chapter 4 for help with setting up your morning routine.)

How many days per week should I work out?
I recommend every day. Why? If something comes up on one or two days and it keeps you from working out, you still get in five or six workouts. If you only plan to work out three days per week (the minimum for keeping fit) and you miss a workout, then you don't get in that bare minimum. An effective workout can be done in as little as twenty minutes, so just do something each day. Really, you should work out every day that you want to feel good!

How can I get my abs back?
You might think you need to do a million sit-ups each week, but actually your abs are affected by what you eat and drink as much as (if not more than) any exercise. Eat clean foods, plenty with high fiber. Stay away from processed sugar and alcohol. (See chapter 7 for more about healthy eating.) Drink at least eight 8-ounce (235 ml) glasses of water every day (more with exercise, pregnancy, and nursing). For the fitness part, I recommend living in plank. Ha! I mean that your abs are always active. Engage! Move from your core. And yes, planks, side planks, crunches and reverse crunches work, too. Perform these three to five days per week.

What types of workouts should I do?

Ones that you enjoy. If you don't like going to the gym, then don't. Here is a list of alternative workouts.

+ Hike
+ Walk your dog
+ Play a sport
+ Go swimming
+ Do yoga
+ Take a spin class
+ Try boxing or kickboxing
+ Use workout DVDs
+ Go to a FIT4MOM class

No matter what exercise you choose, try to mix it up. Do cardio a few days per week, strength training two or three days per week, and keep flexibility as a regular part of the mix. Intensity is important. If your walk or hike is so easy that you can talk to your girlfriend without losing a breath, you need to turn it up a notch!

My personal workout routine looks like this:

+ Monday: Body Back HIIT workout (cardio, strength, and flexibility)
+ Tuesday: Run
+ Wednesday: Body Back HIIT workout (cardio, strength, and flexibility)
+ Thursday: Run
+ Friday: Strength training in my garage (A circuit of squats, push-ups, pull-ups, sit-ups, jump rope, and lunges)
+ Saturday: Yoga
+ Sunday: I take this day off unless I missed a day during the week

Keep It Simple

If your brain came to a screeching halt sometime during this chapter because you felt overwhelmed by the idea of exercising every day, I will sum it all up here. If you want to get specific with your exercise and plan your workouts, you will see the benefits for sure, and you will learn to appreciate the discipline. If it all seems like too much to you, remember this: Move a little every day. Then move a little more. An object in motion stays in motion. Just get started and you will probably want to keep going!

The key to exercising for life is to make it part of your life. You cannot cheat exercise. If you omit it from your life, it will catch up with you later. You say you don't have time now, but I can assure you that physical therapy or rehab from a health condition takes a lot more time (and it is a lot less fun). Find exercises that you enjoy and that you can build upon. You can take baby steps to anywhere you want to go. As Nike says, Just do it!

What at three types of activity that you like?

_____

_____

_____

Look at your schedule. How can you add fitness into your life?

M _____

T _____

W _____

T _____

F _____

S _____

S _____

Your body is your greatest tool. Please, please consider keeping it in shape. It will reward you for years to come.

August:
Plan your workouts. Add one day per week, and/or increase the intensity of your current workouts.

Stop striving for perfection. Strive to be better than you were yesterday.

Don't just go through this year. Grow through it!

Chapter 9

Your Healthy Home

As we talk about the health of our bodies and our families, we can't overlook the effect of the environment on our well-being and health—and our effect on the environment. Our children encounter some 2,000 chemicals each day. They are in our food, our air, and our homes. In this chapter, I will teach you easy steps that you can do and share with your children so they understand how to create and live in a healthier world, starting at home.

Local and Global

Our children are the future. I know you've heard that so many times, but this time I want you to really pay attention to it. Our children are the future, so we need to make sure that they are healthy and that the environment they live in is also healthy. We can't afford to look the other way. Let's start with what we need to pay attention to locally, and how we can make a difference around our home.

Raising Your Green Family

According to the Environmental Protection Agency (EPA), there are more than 80,000 chemicals on the market and less than 1 percent have been studied for safety. Reports have found hundreds of toxic chemicals in babies at birth because pesticides, flame retardants, toxic makeup, shampoo, and other products are all passing through to our babies in utero. We have no idea what kind of damage this can cause to their brains, their immune systems, or their reproductive systems. And I hope we stop giving the world another chance to find out.

The average American has 400 to 800 chemicals stored in their fat cells. The number of immune disorders, neurological disorders, allergies, and hormonal imbalances is skyrocketing; these dysfunctions are often attributed to environmental and lifestyle factors. The situation is concerning enough that entire organizations—such as Healthy Child Healthy World—have been founded to protect children from toxic chemicals in our environment.

But it's not up to organizations to take care of our children and our families. It's up to us. I think it's time we talk about detoxifying our homes, making positive changes in our day-to-day lives to raise a "green" (environmentally friendly) family. We talked about toxins in our foods in chapter 7. Now, let's focus now on the products in our homes.

Create a Green Routine for Personal Care

Is your beauty routine toxic? You would think that your beauty products have to be tested for safety, right? Nope. The Food and Drug Administration (FDA) does no safety reviews on beauty products. The cosmetic industry is totally self-policed, leaving the policing up to us. It's time for moms to embrace the role of being the Green Police for their families.

You might think a few beauty products here and there aren't enough to pay attention to. Consider this: The average person uses nine products on their body daily, averaging a total of 126 ingredients *per day*. Toothpaste, soap, cleanser, shampoo, conditioner, hair gel, hairspray, moisturizer, foundation, perfume, deodorant, sunblock. Are you sure they are all safe, for your kids and for you?

We need to be concerned about the air we breathe and what touches our skin. Your skin is transdermal, allowing things to pass right through it into your body. This happens so easily that some medicines are even given through the skin. Think of how easy it is for other products to pass through as well. While we can't (and don't want to!) keep things from passing through our skin, we can choose to limit the chemicals we use in our beauty products. I'll get you started with some lists of products and ingredients to avoid whenever possible.

Product Beware

The Environmental Working Group (EWG) has an amazing website, and it helps me figure out what products are safe. Through them, I know to be careful about the following ingredients in my products.

AVOID FOR ALL AGES

- Soap
  - triclosan
  - triclocarban
- Sunscreen
  - SPF above 50 (They contain higher concentrations of chemicals and may pose health risks when they penetrate the skin.)
  - retinyl palmitate
  - aerosol spray
  - powder sunscreen
  - oxybenzone
  - added insect repellent
- Nail care
  - formaldehyde or formalin in polish
  - the "toxic trio" in polish: dibutyl phthalate (DBP), toluene, formaldehyde
  - If you're pregnant, skip nail polish completely.

Children are even more susceptible than we are to the dangers of our products. They are often exposed to the same amounts and products as adults, but pound for pound, they can handle less. Their immature systems are not able to fend off many of the toxic ingredients.

AVOID FOR YOUNG CHILDREN

- Baby wipes
  - bronopol
  - DMDM hydantoin
  - fragrance
- Diaper cream
  - BHA
  - boric acid
  - fragrance
- Toothpaste
  - fluoride until you are sure your child won't swallow the toothpaste

Another great website is the Campaign for Safe Cosmetics. (See page 221 for a link.) They have in-depth information about the chemicals to avoid and the products that are safe. The following are common ingredients that you should avoid whenever possible. Below is an abbreviated list from their "chemicals of concern list."

Phthalates: Chemical plasticizers that have been used since the 1950s. Basically, phthalates soften plastic without leaching to the plastic... so they do leach to whatever they are in. For example, they keep nail polish from chipping and hair spray from being too stiff. They make your fragrances last longer. They are in everything from lotions to toys, electronics to plastic containers. They are even on the teethers that our babies suck on!

We are not 100 percent sure about the risks of phthalates, but evidence indicates that they are associated with asthma, early onset puberty, and kidney and liver cancer. Those sound to me like good enough reasons to avoid phthalates!

Parabens: Prevent the growth of microbes. Parabens are found in a huge array of personal products, and they can be absorbed through skin, blood, and the digestive system. They are linked to endocrine disruption, cancer, development and reproductive toxicity. Luckily, it is becoming easier to find products that are paraben-free.

Triclosan: Antimicrobial agent (reduces bacterial contamination). Triclosan has been linked to hormone disruptors, and to bacteria resistant to antibodies and antibacterial products. The Centers for Disease Control and Prevention have identified triclosan in the urine of 75 percent of people tested, a pretty clear indication that triclosan accumulates in our bodies.

Toluene: Toxic chemical used in nail products and hair dyes. Exposure to toluene can result in temporary issues such as headaches, dizziness, and

YOUR HEALTHY HOME

cracked skin, and more serious issues, such as reproductive damage and respiratory problems.

Unfortunately, you cannot avoid all of the chemicals that we are assaulted with daily, so do what you *can* do. Take care of your health where you do have control. Moms can be a catalyst for change, and I hope that more moms will consider being a voice for change toward healthier, greener products in the home.

Love Your Environment

Let's take a break from the chemicals for a bit here to talk about a different way of loving your environment: caring for the space in your home. Clutter, mess, and disorganization can all become toxic to your mental health and even to your physical health. Does that sound a little extreme? Maybe, but trust me on this: Your home space matters more than you probably realize.

"Lisa, clean up your room." Mom would often say this to me when I was a kid, and I remember thinking it would be so much easier if there was a custom space where each toy went. But there wasn't, so I piled things away and shoved them in drawers until my room was seemingly neat. Ah, much like my daughter does now.

If you visit my house, you might be surprised to know that tidying doesn't come naturally to me, because my home is quite neat—most of the time. Keeping tidy has always been a chore for me, but I love a neat and tidy space so much that I do the work to keep it that way. I have learned the importance of loving the space you live in, no fancy house required.

Almost everyone loves a tidy home—whether they have one or not—but for some reason, few of us have actually been taught how to tidy up efficiently and effectively. We might have learned to cook or to sew, but getting organized and neatening up? Not so much. I certainly wasn't taught about organization, so I'm always looking for the secret to staying organized. I have an entire board on Pinterest dedicated to organizational inspiration. I tidy. I get organized. And then somehow everything is messy again.

When I heard about the book *The Life-Changing Magic of Tidying Up: The Japanese Art of Decluttering and Organizing*, by decluttering master Marie Kondo, I had to read it right away. Maybe I could finally learn the secret to getting and staying tidy! I was intrigued to find out that Kondo's system is so effective that, she says, you only have to do the process once. Once? That sounded quite amazing, especially because that drawer in my kitchen seems to become a mess, like, a day later.

Kondo's decluttering and organizing philosophy can be summed up in just two statements:

+ Discard everything that does not "spark joy," after thanking the objects that will be discarded for their service.
+ Do not buy organizing equipment. Your home already has all the storage you need.

I admit that I wanted to start tidying up as soon as read a few pages of the book, but I forced myself to finish reading first. I wanted to make sure that I understood the full concept. If you read the book, I recommend you take the same approach.

Why should you care about this? Because when your space is neat, you can find peace. I remember in college that I would always need to clean my desk before I tried to study or I wouldn't be able to concentrate. Your mind can't be settled when there is clutter around you. When your space is neat, your mind can fall into place and relax.

> *Clutter has only two possible causes:*
> *too much effort is required to put things away*
> *or its unclear where things belong.*
>
> —MARIE KONDO

Kondo believes that tidying is an event, so you need to make sure you have time to tackle it. Also, like most organizing wizards, she suggests the following approach:

1. Bring all items of the same type into one place. You know, for example, how you have clothes in multiple closets? Well, I do. Take everything out of the closets, and bring them all to one place (your bed, for example).

2. Hold each item. If the item sparks joy, keep it. If you remember that it itches, or is out of style, or never hangs quite right, get rid of it. Do not keep clothes that you hope to one day fit in! Those items tell you that you aren't enough right now, and you certainly don't need that negative energy. Be prepared to get rid of a lot. I got rid of five bags of clothes; many were perfectly beautiful, but they were no longer bringing me joy. I'm releasing them so they can bring joy to someone else.

3. Fold clothing carefully. Kondo is adamant that you get the folding exactly right. I have not yet mastered this, so I will spare you the lesson. I do, however, think it is pretty amazing, so I recommend watching a video showing her folding technique: Just search "Marie Kondo folding technique" and more than a thousand videos will pop up!

According to Kondo, you can't just de-clutter. It must take place in a certain order!

- ☐ Clothing
- ☐ Books
- ☐ Papers
- ☐ Miscellaneous
- ☐ Mementos (including photos)

I have one trick that I use for the miscellaneous papers that seem to get strewn throughout the house. Get one big, pretty basket. It is your inbox. All papers go in there. I'm talking mail, bills, kids homework, everything. The trick is to go through it in ten minutes once a day. Deal with anything that can be dealt with in two minutes or less, toss what you can, or keep it in there until you next sort through it. You will never be looking for a paper again as you will know it's in there or filed appropriately. This is a trick I learned from David Allen, author of *Getting Things Done.*

Marie says that we have so much clutter because we hold on to too much. We hold on to things that no longer bring us joy. Look around. How many items do you not even notice? Do you hold on to an item because you may one day need it? Or because you have a memory attached to it? Think about your closet. Your garage. Your junk drawer. Come on, we all have at least one. Cabinets. Book shelves. How many of those things do you really need?

Jason teased me and said I didn't need to read the book because he could have told me that I just needed to get rid of all my extra stuff. I guess the truth is that we all have too much stuff. And we don't like to get rid of it because it seems wasteful. We all probably need to be far more protective of allowing more stuff into our house. Think about your kids' rooms. They get so messy because they have so much darned stuff. We keep allowing them to add more without making them give anything away. At least not at a one-to-one ratio.

Teasing aside, my husband is one of those naturally neat people. Our garage is something to be seen. And you should see his side of the closet. His side never gets messy like mine. It stays neat. That's because he takes care of something right when he sees it, whereas I don't put it away until it seems like more of a priority. Put it away every time, right away. Pretty basic concept, I guess.

But I think that loving your space is more than just being neat. Your space should bring you joy. Peace. Don't wait for another house or new furniture or more things. You can have it right now. One of my very good friends, Annie Fonte, is the creator of a very special life program called Meet Me at the Barn (meetmeatthebarn.com). She lives on my dream ranch, but it's not the horses or the gorgeous home that make it magical. What makes the space special is that Annie surrounds herself with things that she loves. You can hang a picture, post a quote, light a candle, or leave out a memento that will bring you a happy memory.

If you look at a space in your house and it makes your brow furrow because it is cluttered and messy, then you need to deal with it. That is bringing you negative energy every time you pass by.

Annie introduced me to a wonderful website called The Quiet Place. I highly recommend taking some time to check it out (thequietplaceproject. com). Annie gave us all the homework to create a quiet place in our home. One little nook or cranny that gave us peace. We should all have a place in our home to feel comfortable. To feel safe. I set up a spot in my home office. I sit on a couch that has some beautiful pillows. I brought in a statue that has three women meditating. I have some books that make me happy, a plant to give me oxygen, and a candle. This is my special spot to meditate each morning.

My peaceful places have grown throughout my house. Why shouldn't I have things that make me happy everywhere? I have an aromatherapy diffuser in my bedroom. I have pictures that make me happy everywhere. I even have one in my closet. I have a quote that inspires me on the back of my bathroom door. On a bookshelf, create a shrine of mementos that bring you joy. Your home should make you happy.

Sanctuary Exercise

In the space below, design your sanctuary space. What objects would be in it? What objects need to be cleared away?

- Light a candle at any time of day, even when you are getting ready in the morning.
- Play music that soothes your soul or gives you energy.
- Turn off the TV. That noise is probably sapping your energy.
- Use some aromatherapy.
- Create a peaceful ambience in an ordinary day.

I hope I have inspired you to declutter and to find some ways to love your space.

BABY AND TODDLER CAVEAT

Now, if you are a mom to a baby, especially a toddler, then all bets are off. I have never had so much trouble keeping a neat house as when I had little ones running through the house. They seem to leave a trail of mess. I do believe wholeheartedly that it is far more important to enjoy them than it is to have a neat house. The time with them is fleeting. See if you can get some big baskets to throw the toys in. And then find one nook of the house for yourself that is your special place.

Is Your Space Toxic?

Now that we've addressed the clutter and disorganization of a space, let's go back and look at the other kind of toxins that finds its way into your space: chemicals. If you are like me, you might feel pretty overwhelmed as you learn about all the things in your home that might be toxic. Take a deep breath. Now, one more. The first step is education. Learn as much as you can from different sources, then plan out and take baby steps to get your home healthier. (Remember the Kaizen approach? Read chapter 4 again if you need a refresher). I'll help you get started with this list of simple replacements you can make.

For a quick way to green your home space, look for the following items and make the recommended replacements.

- **Nonstick pans.** Replace with stainless steel, glass, or cast iron. Why? Nonstick pans are coated with a toxic chemical.
- **Plastic containers.** Replace with glass (preferred) or BPA-free plastic. Why? Bisphenol A (BPA) and phthalates leach into food. These are associated with cancer, as well as brain and behavioral changes.
- **Canned foods.** Replace with glass-jarred foods or BPA-free cans. Why? The BPA leaches into the food. See above.
- **Cleaning products.** You can make your own cleaners with baking soda, vinegar, and essential oils, or purchase healthy products such as Seventh Generation, Method, and Meyers. Why? Most household cleaning products are toxic, containing phthalates, synthetic fragrances, ammonia, chlorine, and toxic fumes.

Using any of these items a handful of times will probably not cause a problem, but we simply don't know what happens over a lifetime of use. We also don't know what the effects are of using these chemicals in combination. Most of your cleaners have labels that warn the products are dangerous when ingested, touched, or inhaled. I think we need to take those warnings more seriously!

Confession time. This is an area where I'm a work in progress. I'm sure I have jars with BPA and pans that are nonstick. But knowledge is power. The more I learn, the more I know I need to continue to take the toxins out of my home.

To learn more about making healthier and more environmentally friendly choices, see Environmental Working Group (ewg.org).

Protect the Environment

You've probably heard a lot of conflicting stories about how much humans can affect the climate. I know that protecting the environment can seem like more effort than you can spare for something that probably won't make a difference anyway. But think for a minute back to chapter 5, where we talked about shifting focus. It's so easy to get discouraged with a job as big as taking care of our global environment, so let's stop looking at what we can't do and start focusing, instead, on what we can do. Each of us has a responsibility to reduce our carbon footprint (negative effect on our environment). As moms, we have an extra incentive: our children and their future.

FIVE SIMPLE WAYS TO LOVE THE ENVIRONMENT

1. Get rid of junk mail. Did you know that the energy used to produce, deliver, and dispose of junk mail produces more greenhouse gas emissions than 2.8 million cars? Join 41pounds.org/givingback to reduce your junk mail. They stop your catalogs and junk mail.

2. Buy a fuel-efficient car. Or, if that's not financially feasible right now, at least keep your tires properly inflated and keep to the speed limit to reduce emissions. And, of course, carpooling helps a great deal!

3. Use compact fluorescent light (CFL) bulbs. CFL bulbs use about 70 percent less energy than incandescent bulbs. They might be more expensive up front, but they can save you between thirty and eighty dollars in electricity costs over the life of the bulb.

4. Use Energy Star appliances. Look for the Energy Star label, signaling that the appliance has great energy efficiency.

5. Reduce. Reuse. Recycle. Yes, you have heard it before, but it is tried and true!

Environmental Exercise

None of us can do everything, but all of us can do something.

What three things are you committed to doing to improve the environment?

1. _____

2. _____

3. _____

Moms are so skilled at caring. Use that skill to teach our families to care about the environment. Make it fun, make it a contest, and—by all means—make it a habit.

September :

Choose one room in your house and make it your sanctuary, a space that makes you feel happy and at peace.

Stop striving for perfection. Strive to be better than you were yesterday.

Don't just go through this year. Grow through it!

Chapter 10

Strengthen Your Family Bonds

As much as I encourage you to value the me in mommy, the fact is that you are a mom because you have a family and they are important to you. But do your actions actually show that to them? Your family feels important when you set aside time for regular family meetings, dates with your spouse, and time with your kids. In this chapter, I will give you ways to bring your family together and strengthen them as you are also taking care of you. A secret to happiness is giving to others. So, bringing your family together will help you all appreciate your special time and bring more joy into your lives.

Get Real, Then Go Back

Close your eyes. Okay, I get that you can't read when you close your eyes. Read a bit further and then close your eyes. Think about that first time you held your child. Remember as much as you can of the feeling and the thoughts you had.

When you held that new baby in your arms, you had visions of the gifts you wanted to bestow on that little bundle—not gifts you buy, but gifts of life and love. You pictured who you want them to be.

But life happens. Dirty diapers to dirty rooms. Toddlers to tantrums. And then they are teenagers. In that chaos, it's easy to forget the gifts we wanted to share during their childhood. We look at our phones when they play on the playground. We are on Facebook during their practices. We allow the TV to be on during dinner. I get it! It happens to all of us. We all say we value family, but our actions don't always match that intention.

We need to come back to the gifts of life and love that we wanted to bestow on our children. My son Jacob is fifteen at the time of writing this book. He's a sophomore in high school. I conceivably only have two more years with him at home to have an effect on who he will "be." Have I done enough to show him what's most important in life?

Exercise

When you held your new baby in your arms, what did you want your family to be about? Write it all down.

_____

_____

_____

_____

_____

_____

_____

_____

_____

Read again what you wrote down about what you wanted your family to be about. That list is the beginning of your family mission statement.

FAMILY MISSION STATEMENT

I run my family much like I run my business, so it is natural for me to make sure we have a family mission statement. I wanted to create it myself because I know what I want my family to be about, but that wouldn't have modeled very good leadership. Instead, we did it as a family activity during one of our regular family meetings (more about that later). I recommend getting clear on what you want for (and from!) your family, so you can share those hopes with them and help facilitate the discussion.

One way to think about a family mission statement is to ask yourself what gifts of life and love you want your family to have and to share. In the book *The 10 Greatest Gifts I Give My Children*, author Steven W. Vannoy uses the concepts of "gifts" to help us rekindle those values we first wanted to raise our children by. I'll summarize five of them here.

1. The Gift of Living Fully. Vannoy says, *"Children will only escalate their behavior when we force them to deny who they really are or what they are really feeling."*

We need to honor our children's feelings and not try to control when or what they should feel or not feel. As moms, we also need to experience our own feelings fully as we model who are as individuals. Ask your children questions such as, "How do you feel about this?" and "What do you think we should do?" instead of telling them, "Don't cry," and, "You're fine."

2. The Gift of Self-Esteem. Vannoy says, *"When you have high self-esteem you are nearly invincible. No matter what happens, you still know that you are a good and capable person, that you can do what you need to do again and even better."*

Healthy self-esteem is the best defense your kids have in a cruel world. Show encouragement and let them build competence. This means helping them succeed and allowing them to fail. Help your children find something that they are good at and can master. Keep suggesting new activities until they find something that they are proud of.

3. The Gift of Compassion. Vannoy says, *"… being compassionate means coming from a special place in your heart and mind, appreciating and valuing everything and everyone's place in the grand scheme of life. I know that's difficult some days, so be compassionate with yourself, too, and acknowledge yourself for doing as well as you are."*

We must teach our kids to care, to be gentle with others, and to see things from another's point of view. Of course, we must model the kinds of behavior we expect our kids to emulate. Let them see you respond to a variety of situations with patience and kindness, and let them see you willingly help out someone in need.

4. The Gift of Balance. Vannoy says, *"I want to set a model of balance—emotional, physical, spiritual, and intellectual balance. I want them to know that the journey of life includes both pain and joy, work and play. Each one teaches you about the other. They all keep a life healthy and productive."*

Hmm, this sounds familiar. We are our kids' model, so we must live how we want them to live. Let your children see you take breaks, play, and live fully alive. If you lose your temper, acknowledge if you have been working too hard and neglecting your own self-care; this is one of the most valuable lessons they can learn from you!

5. The Gift of Humor. Vannoy says, *"Ah, the gift of humor. Not teasing, not taunting someone because they're different or less powerful, but a genuine expression of joy at the pleasures and ironies and foibles of life."*

A genuine expression of joy. When was the last time you expressed deep-down JOY, that feeling that bubbles up from keeping your life in perspective and balanced toward the positive? Don't have time for joy? Please reread chapter 3.

Laughter is one expression of joy that renews our soul and is actually good for our health. Humor adds color to the day, and it helps you enjoy the process of living. Kids who grow up without a sense of humor live in a state of fear and defensiveness, the opposite of the love and courage we want for them. We must help our children find the humor in the world, without resorting to teasing others. Let your kids see you laugh at yourself and not take the world quite so seriously. Time for another confession. This one is hard for me. Jason and I are both pretty intense people. We probably err on the side of being too serious. So, we have to put effort into bringing some levity and humor into everyday life.

Don't let life get in the way of joy. Don't let busy-ness get in the way of sharing what you value with your kids. If you want to go deeper and learn the other five gifts, read *The 10 Greatest Gifts I Give My Children*. My copy of it is yellow and tattered. It's one of those books that I keep coming back to as a reminder of the gifts I want to share with my children.

My family mission statement is based on the gifts I want to give and receive:

"Be Your Best, Give Your Best, Do Your Best"

Be Your Best: This is the core of who you are. Showing up as your best self.

Give Your Best: Giving is a hot topic in my family. I want to encourage my kids to look for ways to give, whether through charitable work or a kind gesture at the supermarket.

Do Your Best: We don't care if our kids are on the honor roll or are star athletes. We care that they do their best work, all of the time, in all things.

This mission statement might make my kids' eyes roll. Yes, they were a part of creating it many years ago. But it often comes up when a family member is not living up to our agreed mission. It gives us a common language. I may be wrong, but I bet they will tell their kids about it one day, and maybe even create their own family mission statements.

Exercise for Your Family Mission Statement

Do this exercise with your family. Make it fun. Go get a big piece of poster board and pull out the colored markers.

Write down all of the value words that resonate with your family.

What themes are coming up? What is most important, above all else, to your family?

Craft this into a simple, meaningful statement that works for your family.

FAMILY MEETINGS

At some point, I realized that I was actually better at running my business than running my family. I always had time to communicate with my employees, but I rarely knew what was going on in my own household. So, I started holding family meetings in my own home, every Monday night.

Before I explain more about family meetings, let me suggest you purchase a notebook or journal that you use specifically to capture your family calendar, goals, and conversations. Ours includes our family mission statement, New Year's resolutions, and notes from family meetings.

I find that family meetings are a great place to take a pause, sit down, and communicate—something that doesn't naturally happen with two working parents and busy kids. In family meetings, kids learn about planning, problem solving, and listening. I take notes (in the family notebook, of course) on what issues we are having and who is committing to what. This record comes in handy when we forget about changes in allowance or chores, or when we want to review anything else we discussed. While this may seem formal to you, it's actually a wonderful keepsake journaling the growth of our family.

Each year, we use one of our family meetings to write down our New Year's resolutions. When my kids were younger and didn't know how to write yet, they drew pictures of their goals. It's important to let your kids choose what is important to them; one time, for example, my son's goal was to "not bother sister so much." It's truly amazing to look back and see what mattered most to our kids over time. Goal setting with your kids isn't about making sure you create Ivy League scholars or professional athletes. It's simply a great way for them to learn how to change their plans if they didn't accomplish their goals and how to create a new plan for the next goal.

You might be thinking "oh, that'll never work in my family!" when you picture your own family meeting. I should tell you that it never goes quite as smoothly as it sounds on paper. They might roll their eyes and they will definitely complain, so we try to keep it fun. This is a great time to plan fun activities for the month. I even choose a character word of the month for the family to focus on. During the family meeting, we play hangman so the kids can guess the word. Family meetings are also when we give out allowances so that is a definite incentive to participate in the meeting.

Communicating Openly

Teaching communication skills is a big part of our family meetings. It's important that you remain totally quiet until someone is done speaking. We also encourage asking unloaded, open-ended questions. If you can answer with a yes or no, it is closed-ended.

For instance, "How was your day?" will only be answered in fine or good. But "Tell me about your day," should lead to some more open conversation.

Examples of closed-ended questions that parents often ask:

◆ Did you...?
◆ When...?
◆ Will you...?
◆ Have you...?

Open-ended questions encourage kids (and adults) to use language and give fuller answers. Examples of open-ended questions include:

+ Why do you think...?
+ What happened when...?
+ What did you enjoy most about...?

Loaded questions contain a presumption of guilt. They inflame, and they put people on the defensive. "Why do you hit your sister?" assumes you hit your sister. "Why are you so difficult?" assumes something even worse. The most important rule when communicating with your family is to speak to them as you wish to be spoken to.

Stay committed. Eventually, your family will at least get used to having the meetings, and your kids will feel like they are a valuable part in planning your family's days and lives!

We end almost every family meeting with each person in the "hot seat" of positive attention. Each of us tells the "hot seat" person one reason why we love that person. When you are in the "hot seat" you need to sit totally quietly. You cannot say anything until everyone is done speaking.

Family Traditions

Time passes no matter what, but moments can be made more special when you make them traditions. For example, you make a regular breakfast most days of the week, so why not make it more special with a Sunday pancake fun day tradition? Or make the change of seasons something to look forward to by making the first day of spring a day for a family outing. Traditions can be big or small; the only requirement is that they engage your family and are done routinely.

We all want to belong, whether we're kids or adults. Traditions are one way to create that sense of belonging for your family. Aside from having fun together, some traditions teach values through experiences, such as Sunday school, prayers, or going to religious services as a family. Some traditions also connect one generation to another, such as grandparents sharing traditions with their grandchildren and great-grandchildren. These traditions can give everyone in the family something to look forward to, and they help create a lifetime of meaningful memories.

You probably have more traditions than you realize. Do you take pictures of the kids on first day of school? Go to Grandma's house for Christmas? Carve pumpkins as a family before Halloween?

FIVE TIPS FOR CREATING FAMILY TRADITIONS

1. Start small, go slowly. Choose only traditions you know you can stick to. They will lose meaning if you try to do too much.

2. Choose a daily tradition for your family. Maybe a bedtime routine or eating as a family.

3. Choose a weekly tradition for your family. Family game night? French Toast Fridays?

4. Choose an annual tradition for your family. Going to church on Christmas Eve? Working at a soup kitchen on Thanksgiving? A family fun run on New Year's Day? An annual vacation?

5. Don't be normal. What I mean is don't just go along with the usual holiday traditions. Create something that is totally unique to your family. Maybe pick a day of the year that is your family holiday and everyone always agrees to take the day off and do something fun.

Family Tradition Exercise

This exercise would be a great topic for a family meeting. Have everyone give suggestions and everyone gets to vote!

What are your current family traditions?

_____

_____

_____

_____

_____

_____

What new daily family tradition(s) would you like to start?

_____

_____

_____

_____

_____

_____

What new annual family tradition(s) would you like to start?

_____

_____

_____

_____

_____

_____

In today's crazy-busy times, it's more important than ever to use traditions as an enjoyable way to strengthen your family and bring you all closer together!

The Gift of Giving

Me. Me. Me.

Let's face it, we live in a selfie world. I realize much of this book is focused on the ME of mommy, but *you* are an adult who is in very little danger of "over-me-ing." Our children, however, are a different story. One of my biggest concerns for my children is that so many of the messages they hear every day are so self-centered. As parents, we also get a say in what our kids hear, and so it's up to us mamas to help counteract the "me me me" messages. Let's teach our kids the gift of giving.

We all like to receive, and there is nothing wrong with that (within reason). But it really is true that the best gift is in the giving. Many of our kids don't realize this because the gifts that are given today are often quite thoughtless. I admit, I'm guilty of this myself! We grab a gift card at the market for a birthday party. We give cash or some other generic gift that could go to just about anyone. When was the last time you gave a truly thoughtful gift, picked specifically for that person and your relationship with them?

I'm not just talking about gifts that cost money, either. What about leaving an unexpected flower, quote, or a sticky note to inspire someone? How about a card, baked goods, or something special that reminded you of that person?

THE FACTS

Here's what we know about giving:

- ◆ People who give are happier.
- ◆ People who give are healthier.
- ◆ People who give have less depression.
- ◆ People who give live longer.

That sure seems as though giving and volunteering gives back to us just as much as we give away! Let's talk about some more specific giving options.

TOMATO SURPRISE

Have you heard of a tomato surprise? My friend Judy introduced me to this concept. Judy gives everyone at my office little gifts to brighten our day, and she calls them tomato surprises. They're a token, something small, such as a fun pen, favorite coffee, or maybe a plant or a picture. My daughter, Rachel, and Judy have been exchanging tomato surprises for years. They leave small gifts for each other on occasion. Even after all this time, it brightens their day. The best part? The person giving is as excited as the one receiving the gift. Rachel has made Judy pictures, given her a favorite pen, and even made her homemade bath salts. Judy has printed pictures that Rachel would like, and given her tracing paper and colored pencils in a special box. These are the moments we remember, whether young or old. Could you perhaps start a tomato surprise tradition in your home?

DONATIONS

Our kids are going to learn from what we do, so they need to see us give. I have been donating to a charity for years, and I have it set up to auto-donate regularly from my credit card. I recently realized that my kids did not know that I do this, so we talked about it during a family meeting. Maybe you choose instead to give to the homeless person on the corner or con-tribute at your church. Whatever it is, let your children see you give.

> *You have not lived today until you have done something for someone who can never repay you.*
> —JOHN BUNYAN

ALLOWANCE

Speaking of money and giving, we have been giving my kids an allowance since they were little. We have made it a practice from the start to pull 20 percent of their allowance off the top: 10 percent goes to savings and 10 percent goes to charity. This way our children get the reality check that you don't get to keep all of your money, and they learn good habits to start saving and giving.

Ten percent of their allowances doesn't go far, so both kids' contributions go together in a jar. At the end of each quarter, we vote as a family to decide what charity the money should go to. We have donated to animal shelters, Greenpeace, and more. This year, we made a family decision that all of the money will go to Wounded Warriors. When catastrophes have happened such as hurricanes, my daughter has even stepped up and donated her entire allowance to help out.

As you can imagine, your kids might not react to this giving with the joyful heart that you hope for. In many circumstances, my kids have not been thrilled to give. It can be hard to stick to the giving "rules" when the kids are grumbling, but I just keep reminding myself that this is parenting. Some lessons aren't popular, but my hope is that we are raising fine adults, not just happy kids.

> *No one has ever become poor from giving.*
> —ANNE FRANK

TIME

Another way to give is to give your time. I know this is a tough one. There is nothing more precious than time, especially in a mom's life! When you give your time, you give up something that you can never get back. But isn't it worth it? My kids have participated in a great group called Kids Korps (kidskorps.com) where they have had the opportunity to volunteer in many different capacities, including senior centers, animal shelters, and special-needs schools.

As a family, we have volunteered multiple times at the local homeless shelter. One of our favorite things to do is a beach cleanup that is organized monthly by the Surfrider Foundation. I am not sharing this to say how great my family is doing. Truth be told, none of this happens as often or as well as I would like. I am just sharing ideas. I believe that kids who give as part of childhood will be adults who view giving as a natural part of life.

Recently, our family word of the week was *generosity*. We shared with our kids that there are many ways to be generous, using takeaways inspired by my friend Jay Blahnik's speech on living an extraordinary life. Following are some key points from that family meeting discussion.

SIX WAYS TO BE GENEROUS

Note that the main words all begin with a T so they will be easier to remember.

1. **Be generous with your TIME.** Even when it's hard to do, give of your time, your most valuable commodity. My son had volunteered in his sister's class that day, so we used that as a great example. We also noted that Mom and Dad stopping work to play a game is one of the best gifts we can give our kids.

2. **Be generous with your TALENT.** Help out where you have the ability. Examples here ranged from teaching a friend how to make a lanyard bracelet to Mommy volunteering in class to teach fitness.

3. **Share your TREASURE.** For this one, I sat with a big bowl of candy (a shocker to see in my house). I asked my kids how they would feel if I kept it all to myself. "Bad," they said. Then I gave them each a piece, and I asked them if it was really generous if I only shared a piece or

two. After all, I had so many I wouldn't really miss a couple pieces. "No, it's not generous if you won't miss it," they said. So, I shared more of my treasure and my giving made them happy, plus it made me feel good. I explained that to truly be generous, we need to give more than is easy to give.

4. **Be generous with your TEXT.** Being generous with our written words can bring great joy and it costs us nothing. Write kind words in a phone text, write a letter, or leave a love note. Write a word of love on the mirror to your kids and it will make their day.

5. **Be generous with your TALK.** Have you said what you need to say? Our words are so powerful. I want my kids to be purposeful in using kind words and making others feel good. We asked when was the last time that they said something to make someone's day, and we suggested they might call their grandparents just to say "I love you."

6. **Be generous with your TOUCH.** I love this one! A good hug, a held hand, a touch on the back or shoulder—it can be so important as a way to support and connect with someone. Touch can make everyone feel good, young or old, big or small.

Each night of that "generosity week," we asked the kids to tell us how they had been generous that day. Their answers warmed my heart. I hope that maybe, just maybe, it will have a positive, lasting effect on my family.

Monthly Challenge

October:

Purchase a family notebook and set your first family meeting. Create one new family tradition. Choose a charitable activity that you can do together.

Stop striving for perfection. Strive to be better than you were yesterday.

Don't just go through this year. Grow through it!

Chapter 11
Leave Your Legacy

As I already said in the beginning of this book, I truly believe that we are creating a legacy when we parent. Our kids will learn from us, their kids will learn from them, and so on. What an amazing gift and opportunity! Each generation grows a little smarter than the last. We have the chance to live our lives as healthy role models and set the path for positive, healthy lives for our kids, grandkids, and beyond.

Your Legacy, Reprise

Remember at the beginning of the book how we talked about what legacy you want to leave? Let's review this topic, now that you have a different perspective on your life from reading this book.

Legacy Exercise

Again, sorry if this sounds morbid, but how do you want to be remembered? Hopefully, it will be many, many, many, many years from now, but let's ask the same questions again.

How do you want your children to remember you?

_____

_____

_____

How do you want your spouse to remember you?

_____

_____

Your friends?

_____

_____

_____

Keep your answers to this exercise handy so you can use it to guide your Personal Action Plan later in the chapter.

Your Marriage

We have talked mostly about your relationship with yourself and with your kids, but we must not overlook your relationship with your spouse. Most moms tell me their marriage is definitely taking a backburner to parenting. I know it's easy to let the chaos of parenting take over. However, rekindling that romance may be one of the best gifts you can give not just yourself but your kids.

How do you want your son to act toward his wife or partner? How do you want your daughter to act toward her husband or partner? If we want our children to know support, romance, and love, then we need to show them how it's done. Get ready—this is going to be a delicious topic!

Side note: While I may refer to doing things for "him," I am inclusive of all definitions of partnership. Please feel free to change the pronoun if that is a better fit for your life.

DATE YOUR MATE

Think back to when you first started dating.

Remember flirting?

Looking for ways to surprise him/her?

Deep kisses?

Looking into his/her eyes?

Holding hands?

Buying gifts just because?

If that seems like a long time ago, believe me, I understand. I think kids are the anti-aphrodisiac. They are like kryptonite to my sex life. Parenting is exhausting at any age, at any point in a relationship, and the spark gets buried underneath everything else. Unless, that is, you make the effort to get things going again. If you're too tired to figure that one out, just start with the following list.

TEN WAYS TO (RE)CREATE THAT SPARK

1. Give him a ten-second kiss.

2. Put on your prettiest panties and let him know.

3. Leave a surprise note for him in the car.

4. Write him a randy text.

5. Cook his favorite dinner just because.

6. Put a date night on the calendar.

7. Play. Tickle or wrestle even if the kids are around.

8. Take a walk together, holding hands.

9. Have an at-home happy hour to connect before dinner.

10. Have sex.

I can hear you saying you're too overwhelmed to be in the mood, but I'm ignoring that excuse. Dr. Laura, a radio talk show host who specializes in marriage and family counseling, says that if people only had sex when both people were in the mood, then no one would have sex. So do one of these things even if you are not in the mood, and it will create some romantic momentum. Put a date night on the calendar once a month at the very least. Find a way to connect with your partner once a day, even if just for a few minutes. I think you'll be surprised to realize how good it still feels to date your mate!

SHARING THE WORK

Even though lighting that romantic spark will help keep your marriage connected, arguments about workload can snuff out that spark in a heartbeat. Many fights between parents are about unequal workloads, what with taking care of the kids, laundry, cooking, shopping, chores, PTA, and on and on. I think we assume that the goal here is for workloads to be equal, but I wonder if equal isn't the right goal.

I speak to so many moms who get so frustrated with their husbands. "It's not fair," I hear over and over. "We take care of the kids and the house and our own jobs." The workload seems very unbalanced if you keep score.

One of my best girlfriends complains that her husband doesn't cook as much as she does. As much? I would be thrilled if my husband cooked at all. I am not, however, bashing my husband, as he does his fair share of other things. But we definitely don't try for equal.

Instead, we talk about what needs to get done. He is probably not going to clean the house or make the meals, but he helps me by taking care of the cars, insurance, banking, and more. Sheryl Sandberg would say that I need to lean in. She would say that we both participate in bringing home the bacon, so he should take on more domestic duties. Sorry, Sheryl, but I'm quite okay with my arrangement! Jason and I don't look for an even balance. We counterbalance, and we try to cover each other when one person is weighted too heavily.

Neither of you should determine for another what is fair. All that matters is that you and your spouse are happy with your arrangement.

How do you and your spouse handle the responsibilities and chores of family life? Make a list.

_____

_____

_____

_____

_____

Are you both at peace with the division of labor? Consider going over this list together and discussing if any shifts need to take place.

LANGUAGE OF LOVE

How do you make your marriage work? One of the best things I've discovered in my marriage is our love languages. Gary Chapman describes this concept in his book *The 5 Love Languages: The Secret to Love that Lasts.*

Chapman explains that there are five primary love languages of love—"ways that people speak and understand emotional love."

- ◆ Acts of service
- ◆ Quality time
- ◆ Words of affirmation
- ◆ Gifts
- ◆ Physical touch

You might appreciate all of those "languages," but one or two are the primary drivers for you. Where this really matters in a relationship is that we miss the mark when we assume we share the same love languages and we give what we would like to receive. Chances are your primary love language is different than your spouse's.

For example, my primary love language is quality time, so I used to make special efforts to create special times for my husband. The thought was nice, but Jason's primary love language is words of affirmation. By trying to give Jason quality time, I was only speaking my language, not his. When we fought, I might slip and say something like, "You are being a jerk." (I used more vulgar profanity.) That particularly stung for him because words of affirmation are his love language.

On the other hand, when Jason was on his phone while we were having a conversation, it felt similar to him telling me that I'm a jerk. It really hurt. You would think that after years together, we would know each other's primary love language, but no. After fifteen years of marriage, we finally sat down (with a glass of wine) and watched each other take the Love Language Quiz. (You can find a link on page 221.) We were sure we knew how the other person would answer, so when we saw the results we were blown away. Up until that point, we were getting each other's love language all wrong! No wonder we were missing each other's cues.

I now know what is important to Jason, and he knows what is important to me. He even made a list of ways to express love to a quality-time person!

If you're thinking the love languages could also be a great way for you to understand what your kids need, you're in luck. Gary Chapman also wrote *The 5 Love Languages of Children*.

LOVE ESSENTIALS

What are three things that you feel are essential in a loving relationship?

1. _____

2. _____

3. _____

Now before you get all huffy that you are not receiving this in your life, I want to ask you a question. Are YOU giving yourself those three things? It all starts with you! Treat yourself as you want to be treated, and see what happens!

We have talked about the legacy you want to leave, but what do you want your children to carry forward to their own families and future generations? Let's look at some specific questions, not to give you additional work, but as a way to double-check the plans you've made while reading this book.

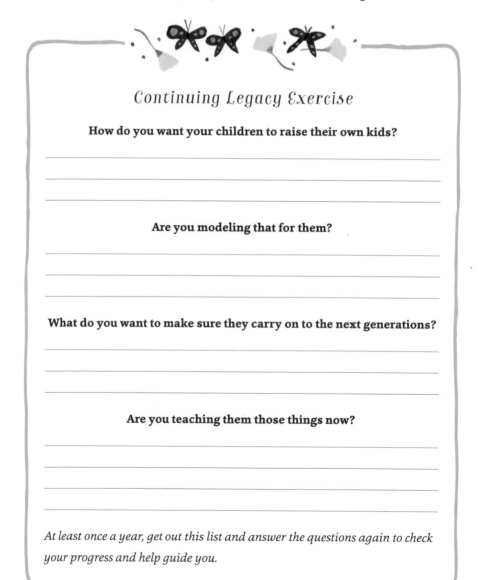

Continuing Legacy Exercise

How do you want your children to raise their own kids?

_____

_____

_____

Are you modeling that for them?

_____

_____

_____

What do you want to make sure they carry on to the next generations?

_____

_____

_____

Are you teaching them those things now?

_____

_____

_____

_____

At least once a year, get out this list and answer the questions again to check your progress and help guide you.

November:

Do the Languages of Love assessment (see page 204) with your partner.

Stop striving for perfection. Strive to be better than you were yesterday.
Don't just go through this year. Grow through it!

Chapter 12
Celebrate!

This is a short chapter, not because it's less important, but because it's a simple celebration of what you've already accomplished. There's no additional overhaul needed, nothing scary to plan, no big risks to take. In this chapter, we will just be grateful and celebrate! I know we don't often think we can take the time to celebrate, but please don't skip this chapter. It matters.

Practice Gratitude

You have probably seen on Facebook or heard from your friends that they're doing a "gratitude challenge" where they come up with three things every day that they are grateful for. If you think that's a wonderful idea, GREAT! Welcome aboard. If you're rolling your eyes, thinking you are SO OVER this gratitude thing, then equally GREAT! We can all use this practice.

I promised I would make this simple, so I'll just say this: The more grateful you are, the more grateful you are. Yes, read that again. When you express your gratitude and your thanks, it grows—even if it's simply acknowledging to yourself that you're grateful about some little thing, such as your kids getting ready for school on time one morning! Remember the Shift Your Focus section in chapter 5 (page 106)? This is the same idea. What you focus on is what you will get.

Let's practice. List ten things you are grateful for, right now. List the first ten things that come up.

1. _____

2. _____

3. _____

4. _____

5. _____

6. _____

7. _____

8. _____

9. _____

10. _____

Notice how you feel after just ten gratitudes. Imagine what a shift you can make if you train yourself to be thankful about more and more things every day.

Take a moment now to decide what one tiny habit you can build into your day to help you remember to be grateful. Write that new habit down.

My girlfriend Farel gave me a gratitude journal. I start every single day by writing one thing that I'm grateful for. Gratitude has been proven to be good for you. Being grateful increases happiness, self-esteem, health, and more. And it's so easy!

I asked some of my friends what they are grateful for and here's what they said.

+ Lynsey W. M.: The health of me:) Thank you, #fit4mom!
+ Shelby N.: I'm grateful to be able to stay home with them, play with them, teach them, and watch them grow.
+ G.G. B.: Their good hearts!
+ Amy H. F.: The ability to be their mom first, but also have a career I love. #FIT4MOM.
+ Erin H.: I am grateful for a husband who understands that as a mom and a business owner, I need time away/to workout/to decompress. And also that he is understanding that my time is important, and that sometimes childcare is needed to help get things done.
+ Joanna B. G.: My espresso machine with buttons to grind and pull the shot. Also that having kids has expanded my community and friend-ships. Children are like the ultimate icebreaker!
+ Rebecca I.-H.: I'm grateful that my children make me want to be a better person, want to work harder to better their lives. I'm grateful my son is so actively talented and secretly likes me cheering him on when he scooters. I'm grateful my daughter is so spunky and full of life that it reminds me not to be so stressed. I'm grateful I have an angel child that may not be here with me, but that watches over me every day and when I feel like life is too much my angel baby brings

me back to reminding all the great I have right here right now. My children make me want to wake up every day and learn something new and play like a child when I only want to be an adult.

- Lee S.: Their curiosity and way of viewing the world in such an innocent manner. Plus the fact that they keep the magic alive by believing in unicorns, Santa Claus, etc.
- Dina C.: I'm grateful they keep me humble! Kids have a beautiful way of making sure your ego is kept in check! It's a good thing!!
- Kristy B. F.: A husband that is crazy supportive no matter what. Watching him as a dad is amazing, and having him support me as both a wife and a mother helps me be better at both of those jobs.
- Katy T.: My village. I'm so grateful for the support of my friends.
- Darcy P.: The fact that I can be as silly as I want with a few people and not be judged!
- Brie M.: I'm grateful for the love I get back from my son!
- Erin B.: My husband!!!
- JoAnn H. F.: The fact that my husband sets a good example for them to become good husbands and fathers in the future.
- Lindsay S.: The random "I love you" that comes out of nowhere but exactly when you need it.
- Jodi D. L.: Lifelong friends.
- Bridget D.: I am grateful that seeing life through the lens of parenthood has made me a better person. All those things that I hope to teach my kids—honesty, integrity, hard work, perseverance—are all things that I strive to be myself, and knowing that they're watching makes me want to do better every day.
- Elizabeth H.: For health and relative prosperity, solid friendships, the challenging team at FIT4MOM, and some amazing authors I visit regularly (blogs & books)—Brené Brown, Seth Godin, Rob Bell, Liz Gilbert, and Glennon at Momastery—who keep me sane and on the right track. And the philosophy of GRIP: approaching people and situations with Gratitude, Respect, Integrity, and Purpose. I am so grateful for my kids and grandkids.

- Becca B.: For finally understanding how much my mom loves me—and being completely overwhelmed by that feeling!
- April S.: How my daughter teaches ME to be nonjudgmental!!! I LOVE HER!!!!!
- Jeannine M.: Having an excuse to act ridiculous. I am grateful that I am fortunate enough to not have to worry about how I'm going to give my children their next meal, or buy them shoes. I'm grateful that my biggest worry is what college my oldest son will get into next year. So many of us living in upper-middle-class prosperity can easily forget about the astounding number of parents who are consistently struggling just to provide the basics for their families. I'm grateful to not be in that situation, and grateful to be able to give my time and money to help those that are and for all of you wonderful parents who do the same.
- Jennifer A. N.: Smiles, giggles, snuggles, and unconditional love.
- Kristin M.: Morning snuggles and the silliness.
- Adrienne F.: That bedtime stories are still "a thing," even as they grow older (and that the stories are much more enjoyable!).
- Caitlin S.: I'm grateful for the way my children see the world and the perspective they provide me.
- Megan A.: Wet baby kisses, good friends, and Starbucks lattes.
- Lauren Alissa P.: I'm thankful that I get to be a "kid" again and enjoy all of the things that we as adults "outgrow" . . . .
- Leah P.: I'm grateful that my husband has a great job that allows us to not worry (or fight) about finances. It allows us to focus on family.
- Adrianne V. T.: I'm thankful for my part-time job that allows me to apply much of the knowledge I worked so hard to gain during college and graduate school, contribute financially to our family, and still be able to spend a lot of time with my kids.
- Rosanna V. B.: I am grateful for not being deployed, but yet grateful for having had that experience as a mother. It really has made me see the little things through a different lens.

- Leanne B.: I'm grateful that I like my kids. I feel like that's different than loving them. They're turning into really neat people that I'd like even if they weren't my own kids.
- Stacey H.: Just being able to have her. It took five years with the aid of many doctors!
- Stephanie G. R.: Maybe corny, but I truly am just grateful that we get to eat fresh, whole foods and have warm beds and coats and shoes. I live in the foothills of the Appalachian Mountains and there are hundreds of families who live in the mountains who have nothing. They are minutes from my door by car. So I think of those families every day when I give my son choices he can have for breakfast. Very grateful.
- Julz A.: That coffee is legal and readily available.
- Ashley V.: I am grateful for my mom. Without her we'd be lost as she keeps my kiddo active and safe while we work to provide.
- Andrea O.: I'm grateful having kids has encouraged me to grow as a person. To break dysfunctional cycles from my family of origin. I was blessed to grow up in a house with lots of love and affection, but no one talked about "the hard stuff." Life is messy. I embrace that and model for my children—that we are all imperfect and can do hard things.
- Irene K. T.: That thirty seconds that the house is "clean" after you've spent hours on it. More importantly ... the fact that snuggle time in the big bed with everybody and the dogs on lazy mornings is a given ... and totally part of our normal agenda. Momma loves her snuggle time and, thankfully, nobody complains about it!
- Lauragail L.-D.: For school days, when all my children are in school and I can go and get a facial in peace.
- Farel H.: Seeing this incredible life every day through my girls' brilliant "lenses."
- Miranda Z.: Grateful for the endless amounts of energy and imagination my boys have.
- Hilary S.: Endless snuggles.
- Judy B.: That it keeps getting better ... just wait 'til you get to have grandchildren, ladies! It's the BEST!

Reflect

Look back at the baby steps you have learned this year. What has resonated the most with you? What do you want to keep working on? The idea was not to have it all perfected. It was to give you tools to live a happy, healthy life as a mom.

Celebrate!

Now that you're in the thankful mode, let's take it one step further to celebration. We all love to celebrate. So why don't we celebrate our own successes more? Celebration is a form of positive reinforcement. You are reinforcing the behavior that you want to see more of. When we celebrate, we take a moment to reflect on what we've learned so we can make a plan to do more of it. Celebration of your successes will help you reinforce a success mind-set—a state of mind that is wired toward success. Celebration will feel good, set off happy chemicals in your brain, and inspire others (hopefully your family). So without further ado, let's celebrate!

Baby Steps Celebration Exercise

Think about the baby-step changes you made this year. Think about how they have added up.

What are some positive differences you're seeing in your life? Write them down.

_____

_____

_____

_____

Well, those are certainly reasons to celebrate!

(continued on next page)

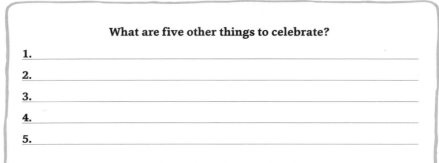

What are five other things to celebrate?

1. _____

2. _____

3. _____

4. _____

5. _____

After any game in sports, the coach will review the wins, losses, gains, and what to do better next time. And they cheer and chant for the win. What if you wrapped up each month with such a review? Check in at the end of each month and review your personal wins, losses, and gains. And where there was progress, celebrate!

I guess we are done. Well, not really done. We are all works in progress. I'm working on life right by your side. I hope this book stays on your nightstand, and it continues to remind you of your most precious life and how you can affect your children by taking care of you!

As we say at FIT4MOM, "the motherhood is real." Yes, the days are long, but the years will go by fast. Yes, it may seem incredibly hard. And I'm telling you to light your fire because YOU are a catalyst for change. There is strength IN motherhood. There is strength in the village of moms.

I believe in the power of moms. I believe in you!

December:

For every day this month, write down one thing you're grateful for. Ask your family members to do the same. At mealtime, share your gratitudes as a family and choose a way to celebrate once a week.

Stop striving for perfection. Strive to be better than you were yesterday. Don't just go through this year. Grow through it!

Resources

BOOKS & ARTICLES

Allen, David. 2015. *Getting Things Done.* New York: Penguin Publishing Group.

Brown, Brené. 2015. *Daring Greatly: How the courage to be vulnerable transforms the way we live, love, parent, and lead.* New York: Avery.

Brown, Brené. 2017. *Rising Strong.* New York: Random House.

Chapman, Gary. 2015. *The 5 Love Languages: The secret to love that lasts.* Chicago: Northfield Publishing.

Collins, M. E. 1991. "Body figure perceptions and preferences among pre-adolescent children." *International Journal of Eating Disorders* 10, no. 2, 199–208.

Davis, Ken. 2012. *Fully Alive: A journey that will change your life.* Nashville: Thomas Nelson.

Ducker, Chris. 2014. *Virtual Freedom: How to work with virtual staff to buy more time, become more productive, and build your dream business.* New York: BenBella.

Grout, Pam. 2013. E^2: *Nine do-it-yourself energy experiments that prove your thoughts create your reality.* Carlsbad, CA: Hay House Insights.

Gustafson-Larson, A. M., & Terry, R. D. 1992. "Weight-related behaviors and concerns of fourth-grade children." *Journal of American Dietetic Association*, 818–822.

Huffington, Arianna. 2015. *Thrive: The third metric to redefining success and creating a life of well-being, wisdom, and wonder.* New York: Baker & Taylor.

Hyatt, Michael. 2012. *Platform: Get noticed in a noisy world.* New York: Thomas Nelson.

Hyatt, Michael S., and Daniel Harkavy. 2016. *Living Forward: A proven plan to stop drifting and get the life you want.* Grand Rapids, MI: Baker Books.

Jordan, Delores, and Jordan Roslyn. 2003. *Salt in His Shoes: Michael Jordan and the pursuit of a dream.* New York: Simon & Schuster.

King, Starla J. 2013. *Wide awake. Every day: Daily inspiration for conscious living.* Little Big Bay LLC.

Kondo, Marie. 2014. *The Life-changing Magic of Tidying Up: The Japanese art of decluttering and organizing.* Berkeley, CA: Ten Speed Press.

McNutt, S., Hu, Y., Schreiber, G. B., Crawford, P., Obarzanek, E., and Mellin, L. 1997. "A longitudinal study of the dietary practices of black and white girls 9 and 10 years old at enrollment: The NHLBI growth and health study." *Journal of Adolescent Health* 20, no. 1, 27–37.

Mischel, Walter. 2015. *The Marshmallow Test: Mastering self-control.* New York: Little, Brown, and Company.

Mogel, Wendy. 2008. *The Blessing of a Skinned Knee: Using Jewish teachings to raise self-reliant children.* New York: Scribner.

O'Brien, Robyn, and Rachel Kranz. 2009. *The Unhealthy Truth: How our food is making us sick and what we can do about it.* New York: Broadway Books.

Olson, Jeff, and John David Mann. *The Slight Edge.* Austin, TX: Greenleaf Book Group Press.

Rubin, Gretchen. *Happier at Home: Kiss more, jump more, abandon a project, read Samuel Johnson, and my other experiments in the practice of everyday life.* New York: Three Rivers Press.

Sinek, Simon. 2011. *Start with Why: How great leaders inspire everyone to take action.* New York: Portfolio/Penguin.

Vannoy, Steven W. 1994. *The 10 Greatest Gifts I Give My Children.* New York: Simon & Schuster.

PODCASTS

Motivating Mom with Lisa Druxman

Happier by Gretchen Rubin

This Is Your Life™ with Michael Hyatt

Youpreneur by Chris Ducker

WEB RESOURCES

FIT4MOM special offers: fit4mom.com/bookinsider

Salary.com Mom Paycheck: salary.com/mom-paycheck

Chore charts: moretimemoms.com/media/pdf/chores-for-kids.pdf

Virtual assistants:
- fiverr.com
- elance.com
- fancyhands.com

Michael Hyatt's Ideal Week: michaelhyatt.com/ideal-week.html

To Do List Apps:
- evernote.com
- nozbe.com
- pomodorotechnique.com
- rememberthemilk.com
- toodledo.com

The KAIZEN™ approach: kaizen.com

B.J. Fogg's research into habit formation: bjfogg.com

Meditation resources:
- calm.com
- insighttimer.com
- headspace.com
- chopracentermeditation.com

Body image and eating disorder information: nationaleatingdisorders.
  org/get-facts-eating-disorders

The Optimist Creed: optimist.org/e/creed.cfm

Brené Brown's TED Talk: ted.com/talks/brene_brown_on_vulnerability

Non-GMO Project: nongmoproject.org/gmo-facts

Tips for heathy eating and meal planning:
  • thefamilydinnerproject.org/resources/faq
  • mommealplanner.com
  • funbites.com

Campaign for Safe Cosmetics: safecosmetics.org

Meet Me at the Barn: meetmeatthebarn.com

The Quiet Place: thequietplaceproject.com

Kids Korps: kidskorps.org

Love Language Quiz: 5lovelanguages.com

MOVIES ON HEALTHY EATING

Colquhoun, James, Laurentine ten Bosch, et al. 2008. *Foodmatters: You are what you eat.* McHenry, IL: Distributed by Permacology Productions.

Cross, Joe. 2010. *Fat, Sick & Nearly Dead.* Brooklyn, NY: Reboot Media.

Fulkerson, Lee, Brian Wendel, et al. 2011. *Forks over Knives.* Santa Monica, CA: Monica Beach Media.

Kenner, Robert, Richard Pearce, et al. 2009. *Food, Inc.* Los Angeles, CA: Magnolia Home Entertainment.

Schwarz, Michael, Edward Gray, et al. 2016. *In Defense of Food: An eater's manifesto.* Arlington, VA: PBS Distribution.

Soechtig, Stephanie. 2014. *Fed Up.* [fedupmovie.com]

A YEAR OF CHALLENGES

January: Commit to ME. Take ten minutes each day to recharge.

February: Choose one section of your Wheel of Life. Give it ten more minutes of time each day.

March: Write down your three MITs each day. Commit to them before anything else.

April: Choose one new habit to focus on this month. Break it down into baby steps, and commit to making one small change daily.

May: Do a "do-over" redirection thought whenever your inner gremlin speaks to you. Do it over as a positive, can-do thought.

June: Create a list of ways you show leadership as a mom. Choose one additional leadership attribute to practice this month.

July: Do a kitchen clean-up. Toss out foods with artificial sweeteners, high-fructose corn syrup, and various CSS (chemical @#%! storm) foods. Start to eat fresh, whole foods at every meal.

August: Plan your workouts. Add a day per week or increase the intensity of your current workouts.

September: Choose one room in your house and make it your sanctuary, a space that makes you feel happy and at peace.

October: Purchase a family notebook and set your first family meeting. Create one new family tradition. Choose a charity activity that you can do together.

November: Do the Languages of Love assessment with your spouse.

December: For every day this month, write down one thing you're grateful for, and ask your family members to do the same. At mealtime, share your gratitudes as a family and choose a way to celebrate once a week.

Stop striving for perfection. Strive to be better than you were yesterday.
Don't just go through this year. Grow through it!

About the Author

Lisa Druxman is a mom on a mission. She is the founder of FIT4MOM (the country's largest fitness program for moms) and a noted speaker, author, podcaster, and powerhouse of energy. A self-proclaimed idea monkey and #momboss, Lisa is passionate about helping women get out of overwhelm and into a life of health and happiness. She shares her life hacks and experiences to help you live a more passionate and purposeful life.

Lisa has appeared on *The Today Show*, CNN, *Access Hollywood,* and *Good Morning America*. She has been featured in print publications including *Entrepreneur*, *Woman's Day*, *Good Housekeeping*, *Self*, *Fit Pregnancy*, and *American Baby*.

She lives and relishes the FIT4MOM mission statement every day, "Helping moms make strides in fitness, motherhood, and life." She resides in San Diego with her husband, son, and daughter, and of course her dog Lexi.

To book Lisa as a speaker at your next event, go to www.lisadruxman.com.